T0065509

Blink Twice For Yes

How a Life Was Transformed by Faith in Jesus Christ

LAURA KLEHR BARNETT

This book is a work of non-fiction. Unless otherwise noted, the author and the publisher make no explicit guarantees as to the accuracy of the information contained in this book and in some cases, names of people and places have been altered to protect their privacy.

WestBow Press books may be ordered through booksellers or by contacting:

WestBow Press
A Division of Thomas Nelson & Zondervan
1663 Liberty Drive
Bloomington, IN 47403
www.westbowpress.com
844-714-3454

ISBN: 978-1-6642-1853-6 (sc)
ISBN: 978-1-6642-1854-3 (e)

Library of Congress Control Number: 2021905260

Print information available on the last page.

WestBow Press rev. date: 3/15/2021

Contents

Dedication

I dedicate this book to the many stroke survivors, and their dedicated healthcare workers, families, and friends. But especially to those survivors who cannot express themselves.

ACKNOWLEDGMENTS

This book has been many years in the making. I wrote about my 1980 stroke and hospitalization between 1989 and 1990 guided by Betty Solyom, my English tutor. She helped put words to my experiences, and she encouraged me to write. I called the work, How Humor Healed Me, but I didn't know the healing process was far from being completed.

In 2010, I moved to McHenry Villa. Because I had used a word processor, the earlier chapters weren't compatible with Microsoft Word on the computer. Marge Zawadzky typed approximately 100 pages of How Humor Healed Me into the computer.

In 2013, I began writing the rest of my story because there was so much more to tell. My friend and advocate, Beverly Meuch, a retired language arts teacher, gave detailed attention to corrections needed in several chapters and, through probing discussions, helped me clarify my feelings and the insights I've gained throughout my journey.

Larry Brook is a retired editor. As we emailed together, his expertise became evident to me in some of the catchy chapter titles he suggested. The book's title was also his idea.

Preface

"It's What's in the Heart that Counts"

In the 50's, there was no such thing as unemployment, and women stayed home to raise the children. Dad worked for a small tool and die company in Skokie, Illinois, a suburb of Chicago.

In 1956 our family, which consisted of Mom, Dad, and six children, lived in an old house in Des Plaines, Illinois. We were five boys and one girl, but that was the year Mom became pregnant with me. It was also the year Dad was diagnosed with ulcerative colitis. At that time, the prognosis for this disease was not good. His boss was very kind, and gave Dad many paychecks when he was sick and unable to work. The surgeon performed a colostomy on him, and he was fighting for his life. Mom came home from visiting Dad at the hospital, and she said to my 10 year old sister Christie, "Your Daddy's skin color is green."

Dad had many hurdles to conquer, but he made it. I know Mom was more than relieved. It would have been very difficult for her to raise seven children all on her own.

I was about seven years old when I had a bad experience at school. Waiting on the little step between the kitchen and dining room, I was looking forward to a talk with Dad as soon as he got home from work. It was usually on what I called my "little step" that my life's problems were solved.

I heard the back screen door open and close, and I hopped up and ran to greet Dad. Before he could get into the house, I cried, "Oh, Daddy!" I grabbed his hand and began pulling him toward our little step.

"Hold your horses!" he exclaimed. "Don't I get a kiss first?"

He bent down, and I kissed him and gave him a big hug. "Daddy, I'm so glad you're home! Can we have a conversation on the little step?"

"Sure," he said, "first let me give your mother a kiss." Mom was by the sink slicing tomatoes for a dinner salad. Dad gave her a hug and a kiss and asked, "How's my bunny with all the honey?"

Giggling, Mom said, "Oh, Bob. I'm fine, but Laura has been waiting to talk to you ever since she got home from school. She had a bad day and she wants to talk ONLY to you."

"Okay, Spooky, let's have a conversation on our little step." Dad sat down on the step and I sat next to him, as he asked, "Now, what happened at school?"

"During recess the kids were making fun of me because I have on red underwear," I explained, sniffling and holding back the tears.

"When people ask me, "What's that bag around your waist? I say that's my money belt, and that's where I keep my millions of dollars."

As he spoke, he tickled me and laughed. When he stopped, he cleared his throat and said seriously, "I'm just rich in love from my family," and tears began to fill his eyes.

I asked, "Oh, Daddy, what do I do when the kids make fun of me?"

His deep blue tear-stained eyes gazed deep into mine. "It doesn't make any difference what you wear," he said. "If you have God in your life, that's all that matters. It's what's in the heart that counts." He pointed at my heart.

"What do you mean, Daddy?"

Laughing, he exclaimed, "Tell them red is your favorite color!"

"Okay," I said. I was so relieved. I jumped up with a big grin and gave him a hug. "Thank you, Daddy!"

That was it! All I had to say was that red was my favorite

color. I now had the ammunition I needed to face the kids on the playground the next day.

Many days came and went. When I became a teenager, Mom and I became very close. It seemed that Dad didn't have the patience for me anymore. Mom said it was because he didn't feel well.

Dad lived for 19 years with the colostomy. He didn't let the colostomy bag hanging from his waist get the better of him. He even went swimming and water skiing while wearing a shirt. He died of colon cancer when I was 19 in 1976.

I was in college when Dad died. After graduating from college in 1978, I met Mike Barnett and we were married. We bought a house in Lake Zurich and were quite happy. I certainly had no idea what was on the horizon for us.

I am writing this book to tell of my journey. At the center of this journey is the strength and conviction I learned from Dad's words, "It's what's in the heart that counts." By sharing my life and its challenges, my purpose is to encourage and bring hope and faith to other stroke survivors and to all those family members and dedicated healthcare professionals who support them.

November, 2020

One

My Life Changer

A voice broke the silence. "Laura, it's time to wake up."

Okay, Mom. Is that you?

"Laura, wake up."

No, you're not Mom. I know you're talking to me because you're calling my name. But who are you? I can't open my eyes.

"Laura Barnett, wake up."

Now, who are you talking to?

"Come on, Laura Barnett. Wake up."

Oh, you must be talking to me. That's right; I'm married now. I used to be Laura Klehr. Now I'm Laura Barnett.

She bent over me cheerfully saying slowly, "Laura, it's June 15, 1980."

Drifting in and out, I suddenly heard the date. *WHAT? Are you nuts? Come on. The last day I remember was May 31.* I formed words to say, *No, it can't be June 15.*

I finally was able to open my eyes, but everything was a blur. The figure scurried about as if not one word had come out of me.

Agitated, I restated, *No, it can't be June 15!*

Once again she didn't even acknowledge me but went right on moving about the room.

I can't believe this! What's wrong with you? Are you deaf? I tried again, trying to scream, *NO! IT CANNOT BE JUNE 15!*

There was no response. The woman-shaped form said, "You're in Northwest Community Hospital."

A HOSPITAL? What for? Hey, lady! What am I in here for?

Ignoring my response, she said it again. This time she said it so slowly that she was irritating me, "You—are—in—Northwest—Community—Hospital."

You must think I'm a real dummy. I heard you the first time. Oh brother! You won't tell me what's going on. What are you? A nurse? Most nurses have the decency to answer when spoken to.

The next day came, and a different female figure said, "It's June 16, and you're in Northwest Community Hospital."

I don't understand how it can be the middle of June already. But, because of their insistent repetition of the dates, it slowly sank in that they had to be right. *These people must really be nurses, but I don't know why I'm in the hospital. I wish someone would tell me!*

I experienced double vision; but more annoying than that, it was blurry and lacked proper depth perception. The floor to the side of my bed seemed to be lying at the bottom of a great abyss, and the ceiling appeared vaulted. Everything in between looked closer than it really was on some days and farther on others. These vision distortions caused my stomach to flutter.

My depth perception problems were evident to me one afternoon when my brother Pete came to visit with Mike and Mom. Pete played his guitar and sang for me. It seemed like they were at the end of a long hallway, and I was in my bed at the top of a high section of bleachers. Though my vision problems were disturbing, the sounds of the guitar and his melodious, gentle voice were pleasing and calming. *I feel so peaceful!* Soon I closed my eyes and fell asleep.

Two

Chop

One day a man entered my room saying, "I'm Dr..." Before he could say his name, I was bawling. He said something, but I couldn't hear him above my wailing. After quite a few minutes, I finally settled down. He sounded impatient as he began again, "I'll be performing surgery on you tomorrow.

Seized by sobbing anew, I thought sternly, *Leave me alone.*

He tried again but couldn't get a word in edgewise with me in hysterics. I'm sure he tried to tell me that I was having surgery and why, but I didn't give him a chance. He probably explained about the surgery, but soon in exasperation, he walked out.

That evening Mike visited. In my confusion, his eyes looked strange and alien. He said, "Laura, you're going to have surgery tomorrow."

Trying to focus on his spooky eyes, I demanded, *What kind? Why?*

He made no response. Mike may have told me I was going to have a gastrostomy, a procedure where a tube is placed in my stomach to feed me, but I somehow got the goofy idea that the doctors were going to chop off my breasts.

Oh no! I've got to get out of here! But my arms and legs won't move! Is that why I'm in the hospital? I can't move anything – not any part of me! The side rails aren't up on the bed! This is my chance! I'm going to get out of here!

Just then a nurse came and put up the side rails of my bed saying, "We don't want you going anywhere."

The nurse must have read my mind! Can people do that here? Is this another planet? It's like someone took my body, put it in a flying saucer that stole my speech and my ability to move, and then plopped me on this bed! HELP! MIKE! SOMEONE – ANYONE! PLEASE, MIKE! ANYONE, COME HELP ME!

Mike had to go and he said good-bye. He leaned over and kissed my cheek. I tried to warn him that I was being carried away to outer space, but no words formed on my lips. He walked to the door, paused, looked back, and then was gone. I was alone.

With the morning light a cheerful voice was again saying, "Wake up, Laura. Wake up."

I opened my eyes and saw everything as one big blur. My hopes were immediately shattered. *Oh no! I'm still in the hospital.*

A nurse said, "It's time to wake up. You have surgery today."

They got me ready, moved me onto a gurney and rolled me down the hallway. I remember the huge spotlights on the ceiling of the operating room, the needle going into my arm, and then I blacked out. The operation turned out to be a success, and by the next day, the thought of having my breasts removed was gone from my mind. Soon, it was on to bigger and better things.

The operation I had was a gastrostomy, the insertion of a feeding tube in my stomach. I got to keep my breasts!

Three

Blink

Mike began, "Now, Laura, we're going to ask you some questions. Blink once if the answer is no, and blink twice for yes."

What a great idea! Now they'll know that I understand what they're talking about.

Mike asked, "Are my eyes blue?"

Trying to focus on them was impossible, but I remembered that they were brown, and I blinked once for no.

He asked, "Are they brown?"

I blinked twice for yes.

The nurse asked, "Is it 1981?"

I blinked once for no.

"Is it 1980?"

I blinked twice for yes, which was correct.

Now Mom asked, "Is Carter the president of the United States?"

This question, I had to think about. Blinking twice for yes, I was correct again.

Mike and Mom left to return to work. Two or three nurses began bombarding me with questions; to all of them I blinked correctly. Excitedly, one nurse exclaimed, "We're going to post a sign by your bed! It will read, 'Laura Barnett seems to understand everything!'"

Big deal.

In fact, a big deal was really about to happen. One day Mike said, "The doctors think you should go to a rehabilitation unit, which means you'll have to go to another hospital. There, they'll have everything to help you get well."

I want to get well, but I want to stay here. I know the staff here, and they know me.

With hopeful expectation Mike said, "I'm going to take a tour of a couple different hospitals. I'll let you know what I think. Is that okay with you?"

Even though blinking was getting easier, it seemed hard to blink this answer. Not wanting to defeat Mike's enthusiasm, I blinked twice for yes, but I thought, *I don't want to go!*

A few days later Mike told me, "I think Lutheran General Hospital in Park Ridge is the best place for you. You'll be put on a waiting list and probably get in by next week."

I blinked for yes.

Then he said, "I wonder if you remember anything about the day this all happened." He asked, "Do you remember planting flowers with our neighbor Tom?"

It seems so long ago. I blinked twice for yes.

"Good," he said. He paused and asked, "Do you remember that it was May 31?"

Again, I blinked for yes.

Mike said, "That's enough questions for right now. I'm glad you remember planting flowers with Tom on May 31. You rest."

I closed my eyes, and thought, *I do remember planting flowers with Tom. . .*

Four

What a Migraine!

I woke up May 31, 1980 to a gorgeous spring day. Mike and I had the day off work, so I was hoping we would get a lot done around the house. Energy whirled through my body making me excited to the brink of giddiness. After a long mid-west winter, the thrill of spring made me feel like a new bride, which I was.

Mike and I had been married a year before on May 12, 1979. In the fall of that year, we had purchased a small ranch house. Besides being a newlywed and a new homeowner, I worked full time at Good Shepherd Hospital in Barrington, Illinois, as a medical technologist in the laboratory. I was almost too busy to enjoy my hobbies – playing the piano, clarinet, and flute, doing needlework, going horseback riding, and snow and water skiing. Mine was, indeed, a full life.

Mike and I worked at outdoor chores all morning. We came back in the house for a break. Mike was in the living room watching TV when I called to him from the kitchen and asked if he wanted lunch before we went back outside.

"Sure, that sounds good," he said from his favorite chair.

I grabbed a package of hot dogs from the refrigerator and put them into boiling water on the stove. We had lunch in our usual manner, Mike relaxing in the recliner, and me sitting cross-legged on the floor by the coffee table as we both watched TV.

When he was finished, Mike snapped the footrest of the recliner down as he came to an upright position. "Well, we better get to work," he announced.

"Yes!" I exclaimed. I hopped up full of vigor.

My first task for our afternoon work was to talk to our neighbor Tom about planting some flowers together. I ran next door and found him already outside doing yard work.

"Hey, Tom, would you like me to go to the nursery and get some petunias? I was thinking they'd look nice over where the gaslight is," I suggested as I pointed to an area where our driveways joined.

"Sounds great, Laura."

"They would definitely add color there," I said. "I'll go pick them up."

"Be sure to let me know how much they are. I'll split the cost with you."

I jumped into the car and called over to Mike, "I'm going to the nursery to get some flowers."

"Okay. I'm going to my boss's house to work on my car for about an hour."

At the nursery, the red and white petunias caught my eye. I bought two flats of flowers and then drove home feeling as if I could conquer the world. My new life was going along smoothly, and I was very happy.

I arrived home and opened the trunk.

"Ready to begin planting?" I called over to Tom.

"As ready as I'll ever be."

We collected the garden tools and began loosening the soil with trowels. Suddenly, I felt dizzy, and I grabbed the gaslight post nearby to keep from falling.

Startled, Tom asked, "What's wrong?"

Grasping my head, I replied, "I feel dizzy – but I'll be all right."

The dizziness subsided, and I knelt down to cultivate the soil some more. Then as I tried to get up and move around the gaslight post, the dizziness returned. I stumbled backward, catching myself before hitting the ground.

Tom, now alarmed, ordered, "Lie down on the grass."

I lay down and closed my eyes to stop the dizziness. I wanted to get up and help Tom, but each time I opened my eyes, the gyro-motion clutched my body and sent my world reeling. When I closed my eyes again, the dizziness stopped.

I heard Mike's car pull into the driveway and felt relieved. He was home, and he would know what to do.

When he saw me lying on the grass, Mike laughed and called over as he teased, "Laura, why are you letting Tom do all the work?"

"You'd better check on your wife," Tom said without humor.

"Laura? Are you okay?" Mike called and ran over.

"I feel dizzy....It must be a migraine headache."

Mike helped me into the house and onto the couch. He sat with me for a while and then went about his business outside. A few minutes later he came in to check on me asking, "Are you okay?"

I didn't want Mike to be concerned, so I insisted, "Don't worry; it's only a migraine." I didn't know what else it could be.

Mike went back outside.

Feeling the urge to vomit, I stumbled down the hallway to the bathroom, scraping my arm on the counter as I passed. I fell toward the toilet banging my knee on the way down. After emptying my stomach in the bowl, I lay down, still dizzy. The cool floor felt so good.

A little while later Mike came in to check on me again and found me on the floor in the bathroom.

"Laura! What in the world is happening? Let me help you back to the couch."

"Don't ... wor-ry," I slurred. "It's. . .only ... a ... migraine." These were my famous last words.

Mike reacted swiftly. "I'm getting help," he said. He went to the phone. He talked to the hospital emergency room for advice several times, but nothing they suggested worked. He was on the phone again when he heard dull thuds coming from the bathroom. He slammed the receiver down and rushed in, finding me in convulsions. Immediately he ran to the house of our other neighbor Dave for help. He frantically called to Dave, "Something's wrong with Laura! Will you help me take her to the hospital?"

Dave raced with Mike back to the house. He took a quick glance at me and gasped, "Oh, my!"

They rushed me to Good Shepherd Hospital only five miles away. Soon I was on an examining table, and I felt my clothes being ripped off. I heard someone say, "She's going to have to go to another hospital. She needs a brain scan, but Good Shepherd is new. It doesn't have a machine. She'll be brought back when she's done."

They loaded me into an ambulance. My head was swimming and my legs were shaking uncontrollably. Before I knew it, the ambulance stopped, and I recognized the antiseptic smell of another hospital. Hearing voices, I assumed they belonged to medical professionals.

Suddenly I was in a tunnel with some kind of a device being moved around my head. I could hear the slow grind of a machine in motion. A woman's voice resounded from the other room, "Hold still . . . hold still . . .HOLD STILL."

It was an impossible task because I had no control of my own body.

The voice urgently repeated itself, "LAURA, HOLD STILL!"

I can't. I'm trying. I'm trying. If you would just listen to me, you'd be able to hear me. Now wait. . .Let me. . .try. . .to. . .think. Yes. . .yes. . .Let me. . .think. Mike and our. . . neighbor. . .. .D a v e. . . took me to the. . .hospital!

The voice drilled through my skull once more, "PLEASE, LAURA BARNETT, HOLD STILL!"

That sentence was the last I heard before I began traveling into a region of nothingness. Having no spaceship, I took the wings of an injured brain to a place where no earthly concerns are important, no material possessions are necessary, and where time and space have no meaning. I was in the coma zone. For two weeks, I lingered there without the slightest conscience connection to the real world.

At the time of that brain scan, I had a blood clot which doctors couldn't see because it was lodged in the basilar artery of my neck, but the scan only showed my head. The diagnosis of Cerebral Vascular Accident (CVA), or stroke, was made three days later.

Currently, one should call for an ambulance because Emergency Medical Technicians or EMTs are trained in the immediate care of a stroke. In addition to a brain scan, the MRI is available which can give the doctors a detailed picture of the whole body. If stroke is diagnosed, immediate action is taken. When the stroke is determined to be hemorrhagic (a brain bleed), surgery repairs the damaged vessel if possible. In the event of an ischemic stroke (blood clot), "clot-busting" medication can be given which, when administered within three hours, can mitigate the physical residual of the stroke, sometimes leaving the patient with no symptoms at all.

After those two weeks of being in a coma, I was plagued by dreams which mixed with reality. The two could not be separated. In one dream, my family was at our summer vacation spot in Wisconsin, and all of us kids were young. Then I was in a hospital room, and my doctor was visiting me in street clothes. In another dream, I was ice skating with Dad. This was so realistic that when Mom came to the hospital to visit me, I wondered, *Where is Dad?* I had forgotten about his passing.

Is what's happening around me reality?... or... just a dream? Those questions continually challenged my confused mind.

Five

Another Hospital

Footsteps coming into my room woke me up.

Where am I? Am I at home?

I saw a strange woman next to my bed.

"Laura, it's June 29 – can you wake up?"

I squeezed my eyes shut and opened them again.

The woman continued, "The note above your head reads that you understand everything, and you blink once if the answer is no and twice for yes. I'll ask you some questions."

That's right. I'm in a hospital. All I can do is blink.

The woman inquired, "Let's see...are you in Northwest Community Hospital?"

I blinked twice for yes.

"Are you in Wisconsin?"

I blinked once for no.

"Are you in Illinois?"

I blinked twice for yes.

"Your husband is coming this morning," she said. "He'll be riding along with you in the ambulance to Lutheran General Hospital."

Right at that moment Mike came in and said, "Hi, Hon. Are you ready for our ambulance ride to Lutheran General Hospital?"

Immediately, I started crying. *I want to stay here! I don't want to go to a different hospital!*

Mike quickly changed the subject. He said, "It's really a nice day outside."

I settled down to a few sniffles here and there.

The paramedics came in with a stretcher to take me to Lutheran General Hospital. They moved me onto their stretcher and began wheeling me down the hall. I began to cry again. *I just started getting used to it here. I don't want to go!*

Mike was walking alongside of the stretcher and said, "Laura, it'll be okay. I'm going with you in the ambulance!"

As I was being wheeled down the hallway, fearful, tense, and screaming, all the unanswered questions of what this new hospital would be like raced through my mind. The paramedics pushed the stretcher, one on each end, while Mike teasingly called out, "Look out! Here we come."

When I continued to cry, he tried to cheer me up saying, "Hey, Laura, we almost wiped out a nurse with your stretcher."

Still, his humor didn't stop my sobbing. *Why can't I stop? I want to, but I just can't.* Finally I calmed down, exhausted, *Mike, why do I still have this blurry vision?*

There was no response from him. All I could identify of him was the faint outline of his dark brown hair, but I could hear perfectly the soothing familiarity of his voice talking to the paramedics.

Suddenly we stopped moving, and I could smell the fresh air of the outdoors. *I'm so upset! Mike told me that I'm going to this new hospital for rehabilitation, whatever that is. I want to stay here! I'm finally comfortable here at Northwest Community Hospital.*

Soon I was being jostled about as the paramedics lifted me into the ambulance. The adventurous boy in Mike asked, "Can you turn on the siren on the way there?"

One of the paramedics hopped in the back saying, "Maybe, if there's a traffic jam."

I heard him rustling papers as he said, "I need to ask one of you some questions." Mike was near the foot of the stretcher as the paramedic directed his next question to him. "She can't talk, can she?"

Mike said, "No."

It's not that I can't talk. I think I can, but every time I try, it takes so much energy that nothing comes out. Then I get so sleepy. Besides, when I do talk, people don't listen to me. What is going on? I'm glad that Mike is here to answer questions for me. I can just lie here. I think I have a migraine headache. What is wrong with me? Why am I in a hospital? I haven't been told why, and I haven't been able to ask anyone. When I get to this new hospital, maybe then I can ask. After all, Mike assured me the people there will help me get well.

"She can't move either?" the paramedic asked.

Mike said, "No. She's only able to blink her eyes."

The paramedic said, "By the way, my name is Jim. How old is she?"

"23."

"Oh, wow!" Jim exclaimed. "Is that ever young! How long have you guys been married?"

"We just celebrated our first anniversary two weeks before this happened."

"Any kids?"

Mike, sighing with relief, said, "No, thank God."

I wonder why Mike is glad we don't have kids. I thought he wanted them.

Jim exclaimed again, "Now this!"

Now what? I only have a migraine. Don't I? I don't know what people are making such a fuss over. Why can't I go home? I don't WANT to talk! Pretty soon I'll feel like it but not now. WHAT IS WRONG WITH ME? Will someone tell me? Maybe I'm dreaming. I sure hope so...

Again I heard some rustling of papers. Jim said, "I need to verify some information."

Okay, now I think I'm ready to answer your questions, Jim. Go ahead and start asking me. Jim was staying near the foot of the stretcher, not even stepping toward my face. *Jim,* I called, *you won't be able to hear my whispers. Come here. I'll answer your questions.*

Without acknowledging me, he said to Mike, "It says here that she was healthy."

"Oh, yes," Mike immediately responded. "She loved horseback riding, water and snow skiing, and a bunch of other sports. She was very athletic!"

Why is he talking in the past tense? I still love those sports!

Jim then asked, "How long has she been at Northwest Community Hospital?"

Mike, let me tell him. These questions are about me. I can answer for myself. I'll talk. If Jim will just come closer, then I'm sure he'll be able to hear me.

Mike answered, "She went to Good Shepherd on May 31 and stayed one night. Then she came here to Northwest Community on June 1st. Let's see, today is the 29th of June, and that's almost a month."

A month? Mike, you don't know what you're talking about. NO! It hasn't been almost a month. It's only been a few days. I'll talk. I'll talk! Sir, please listen! It's only been a couple of days. Believe me, I know! I'd know if I'd been here almost a month. Yet, I vaguely remember a nurse telling me I had been in a coma, but I don't remember being in one. Mike, wouldn't I remember a coma?

He did not respond.

I WANT TO GO HOME NOW!

Again, there was no response.

Jim continued asking Mike, "Was she at Good Shepherd Hospital before that?"

Mike answered, "Yes, for one night."

Well, at least I think Mike got that right. I remember being at Good Shepherd Hospital in the Emergency Room. I don't remember spending the night. Could I have been there all night?

Jim said in a questioning tone of voice, "We'll be going to Lutheran General Hospital in Park Ridge?"

Mike said, "Yes."

It's no use. They won't listen to me. I'll just lie here and close my eyes. Maybe all of this is a dream. Maybe I'm not really here. I hope not.

Jim asked, "Once we get there, what floor?"

Mike replied, "Sixth. Physical Rehabilitation."

My eyes snapped open. *Rehabilitation! There's that word again. Mike told me about that before. What did he say? Oh, yeah. The people there will help me get well. What is rehabilitation? Is it like making an old house new? Are the doctors there going to make me like new? What has happened to me? Why am I going from one hospital to another?*

The driver said, "Okay, away we go."

I don't want to go to another hospital. I JUST WANT TO GO HOME! Please, Mike! Why won't you listen to me?

As we pulled away, I began crying again, but Mike cheered me up with his joking and teasing. We rode for what seemed like a long, long time. Mike crouched by the stretcher looking out the window.

The driver said, "We're almost there. Do you want me to turn on the siren?"

Mike responded enthusiastically, "Yeah!"

The ambulance driver turned on the siren and Mike excitedly reported, "Laura, you should see the cars getting out of our way!"

Six

Laugh Out Loud

When we arrived at Lutheran General Hospital, Mom was already there. Because of my blurry vision, she was only recognizable to me by her silver hair and her opera-singer-like voice as she asked, "How was your ride?"

Mike replied, "Fine. The ambulance driver even turned on his siren. Right, Laura?"

By blinking twice for yes, I agreed with him. Because I wasn't able to make a sound but to cry, or move a single, solitary muscle below my eyes, I was put in a room nearest the nurses' station so they could hear my cries. I cried for all my needs, because there was nothing else I could do!

The ambulance drivers left, and Mike and Mom began to familiarize me with my new surroundings to make me feel at home. Mike looked out the large window on the far side of the room and said, "I can see my car in the parking lot...way down there!"

Mom moved over by the window, looked and said, "There it is." Then she said, "Laura, there are shelves here on the wall. I bet one is for you, and one is for your roommate. I wonder where she is?"

Oh, I have a roommate? It's like I'm in college anticipating the arrival of my new roommate. But wait. . .I'm in a hospital. . .I don't want to have a roommate. It would be different if I could talk. Maybe since I'm in a different hospital, I'll be able to talk to my new roommate.

Mom said, "I guess you'll be on the B side, Laura. It says B on this empty shelf. The other one must have your roommate's stuff on it. I'm putting all your plants and cards up here." Mom walked over to the closets saying, "This closet with a B on it is yours, too."

A nurse walked in and I could tell she was young by her voice; otherwise, she looked like a blob. She said, "Hi, Laura. My name is Marilyn."

Mike and Mom introduced themselves.

Marilyn continued, "I'll be your primary nurse, and whenever I'm here, you'll be one of my patients." The Marilyn-blob moved closer, "Let me see you blink."

I feel like I'm on stage. I'm a dog performing a trick. Here goes the drum roll. Blink once. Blink twice. *Ta – daa!*

Marilyn said, "That's very good. Can you move your right arm?"

Wanting her approval, I tried my best, but I couldn't move it at all. *I was hoping that once I got to this hospital, I'd be alright. No such luck.* With my continual disappointments, my only recourse was to cry.

In order to stop my outburst, Mike quickly changed the subject. This time, he suggested, "Laura, why don't you give Marilyn the 'google eyes'?"

Immediately my concentration went to moving my eyebrows, "Up, now down. Up and down, up and down, up and down."

The Marilyn-blob exclaimed, "That's good!"

Mike added, "You know, Laura. These people here are going to help you get well."

Yes! I'm going to get well! I don't know what's wrong with me, but I know I'll get well. I am determined!

Soon another nurse came in, and Marilyn introduced her, "This is Carolyn."

The Carolyn-blob said, "Hi, it's nice to meet all of you."

Oh, good. She sounds young, too. Thank goodness!

"Laura, are you doing okay?" Carolyn asked.

I blinked twice for yes.

Carolyn said, "Laura, we'll take good care of you." She turned away from me as she asked Mike and Mom, "Do you have any questions?"

Mike and Mom both said, "No."

Marilyn said, "Carolyn is your secondary nurse, Laura. That means, if I'm not here and Carolyn is, she'll be your nurse."

That's nice. They both sound like they're about my age.

Marilyn continued, "Carolyn and I have an apartment together. We'll be able to keep close tabs on you."

Just then a woman in a wheelchair came in saying, "I just got out of therapy." She looked like a blob, too.

Marilyn and Carolyn both said, "Oh, hi, Muriel."

Then Carolyn said, "Laura, this is your roommate, Muriel."

WHAT! Is she in a wheelchair? And is she old? I don't belong in a hospital, not here with old people. Get me out of here! I definitely won't be in a wheelchair. Therapy? What can she do sitting in a wheelchair? I want to go home! I don't even want to TRY to talk to her.

Marilyn said, "We'll leave you alone for your family visit. If any of you need anything, just let one of us know."

They left and Mom said, "Laura, I think you're in a real good place to help you get well."

No, I'm not! Let me out of here! I don't belong here! I want to go home!

Mike and Mom moved two chairs closer to the bed in order to see the television.

Mom asked me, "Do you want your glasses on so you can see TV better?"

They probably won't help much. Ah, why not. I blinked twice for yes, and Mom handed my glasses to Mike. He clumsily tried to put them on me, but his aim was faulty. He pushed the nose piece up my nose! I burst into a loud hysterical laugh, almost like a volcano erupting. The noise shocked me. *Is this me laughing? No! It can't be. I don't sound like this.* It was a husky, guttural, spasmodic laugh, totally unlike my own. *Who else is in the room? I don't know who could be making this weird noise.*

Mike and Mom looked at one another.

Mike asked, "Laura, are you laughing or crying?"

When they saw no tears, they assumed I was laughing and they started laughing, too, which made me laugh harder. *It* IS *funny, but not THAT funny. Why can't I stop?*

Seeing me laugh after two weeks of being in a coma and two weeks more of only blinking my eyes and crying, Mike and Mom continued to laugh.

This, in turn, made me go on and on. When I took in a breath, I made a horrible noise that sounded like a donkey braying. *My sides are beginning to hurt. Oh! I'm actually laughing! This feels so good! I feel like a canary being let out of its cage! I'm a bird set free! I feel I can fly! What fun this is!*

I began to drool. Because I wasn't able to stop laughing, the drooling wouldn't stop either. This hilarity went on and on, and Mike stretched it out by repeating the incident over and over in a clowning manner. *My sides are going to burst.* The uproar continued with the drooling. *I've had enough! My arms are dead weights, so I can't even grab my sides. Ohhhh. . . Please stop!*

Mike and Mom, enjoying the gaiety, kept on.

Finally, we all began to settle down with a few giggles here and there. Mom wiped the drool from my mouth, and Mike was now able to get my glasses on straight.

We all turned our attention back to the TV screen. There was a funny movie on, but I watched without interest. Pretending fascination with it but reliving the glasses scene, I would periodically explode into my new form of laughter.

Mike and Mom thought I was laughing at the TV, but I wasn't.

Then my glasses slipped down my nose. Paralyzed, I couldn't even scrunch up my face to adjust them. So I stared at Mike sitting across from my bed. After a few minutes, he asked, "Is there something wrong?"

I blinked twice for yes.

He hopped up asking, "Are your pillows high enough? Can you see the TV all right?"

I blinked for yes.

He took a quick look around the room and then looked back bewildered.

I was staring down at my glasses, continually raising my eyebrows. Up and down – up – down – up - down.

"Oh," he said, "I think I know. Your glasses are falling down."

Blinking twice for yes, I felt instant relief at being understood.

Skillfully now, he pushed them up, realizing that I wasn't fragile and wouldn't break.

In retrospect, I can see that my first laugh, about four weeks after the stroke, and the many laughs after that have carried me through my life. My laughter was especially important during those many months of challenging therapy. Because my emotions were so tender, I would laugh and cry within the same moment. My laughter and my crying were so explosive that they many times surprised even me when they occurred, but my biggest problem with those emotions was that I couldn't shut them off. Sometimes it took me an hour to settle down from crying and laughing.

I didn't know it then, but this lack of emotional control is a by-product of some strokes. It's called emotional lability or pseudobulbar affect.

Seven

Dr. Lee

Here I am at Lutheran General Hospital, but I don't know why I'm here! It must have something to do with my inability to talk or move. But I don't understand why I can't go home! My thoughts were conflicted, sometimes rational but sometimes not. I had no idea what was going on!

One day, like a small tornado, a tiny Asian woman came bouncing in with a burst of energy, saying, "Laura, I'm Dr. Lee, and I'll be your doctor. How are you, today?"

I blinked twice for "Fine." *Oh, she's a woman. What a relief! Whenever a strange man comes in, I cry, even if he's a doctor. I don't seem to cry with women.*

She asked, "Can you move your right arm?"

Giving it my all, I was able to move it a little. *Look, Dr. Lee! Look! Did you see it move?*

Dr. Lee remarked, "Ah-so."

Wow! Did you see that, Dr. Lee? I'm thrilled! I couldn't do that before!

"Now," she directed, "move your right leg."

Making a big effort, I felt as if I had moved it.

Dr. Lee chanted, "Ah-so," in the same unaffected tone.

I can't tell by your voice whether I moved it or not. Maybe I did, but you didn't see it. I want to show you what I can do. I'll try it again.

I tried to move my right leg again, but in an instant, she continued, "Your left arm."

Wait! I have to think about moving it.

There was no movement and no comment by Dr. Lee.

Dr. Lee continued on, "Your left leg."

Wait, Dr. Lee. You're going too fast! Slow down.

Silently, Dr. Lee bent over my legs, lifting first one, then the other. With a hard object, she did something to the bottoms of my feet. I was puzzled with this maneuver.

Then she told me to close my eyes.

I tried, but they wouldn't close all the way.

This time she reacted only with, "Ah." Then she said, "Stick out your tongue."

I'll try!

Before I was able to give it a gallant attempt, she said, "Ah-so." Immediately she asked, "Can you nod your head?"

Up and down went my head ever so slightly. *I did it! Oh, Dr. Lee! Isn't that great? I couldn't do that before.* I heard a spasmodic laugh that was somehow familiar. I looked around the room to see who was making that strange noise. *Who is that weirdo laughing? Oh, yeah. That's right; it's me! Dr. Lee, why aren't you excited about me being able to nod my head?*

She made no response.

That's right; she has never seen me before. She doesn't know what I can and can't do.

Dr. Lee wasn't the least bit impressed. She continued in her sing-song way, "Ah-so." As she hurriedly left, she waved, saying, "See you later."

Wait. . .Wait. . .Dr. Lee. . .Wait.

She left the door partly open.

Is she coming back? I kept looking at the door. *No, I guess not. Oh, well, I'm just glad that I have a woman doctor. I sure hope that now because my doctor is female, I won't cry. I hate it when I cry, but it just happens. I can't prevent it.*

After a little while, a nurse came in and explained, "You're on the sixth floor of Lutheran General Hospital, and this is a physical rehabilitation unit."

Rehabilitation? There's that word again. What do you mean?

The nurse continued, "This is a special floor. All the therapy you'll need will be right on this floor. The patients here learn to help themselves."

What? What are you talking about? I don't need to learn to help myself. I can already do that.

"And the nurses are all trained to help in your rehabilitation."

Get me out of here! I don't understand what you're talking about!

"Do you understand?"

I tried to shrug my shoulders to let her know that I didn't understand, but I couldn't move them at all. Next, I tried shaking my head. I felt as if I were in a wrestling hold, with my head a block of cement. My head would not budge. When nodding and shrugging didn't work, I reluctantly blinked twice for yes, not wanting to extend this conversation.

"Great. You'll soon learn to become independent."

Independent? I am independent!

The nurse went on and on, but I didn't hear her because I was mesmerized by the monotony of her voice.

What did she say about being independent? I only have a migraine. This migraine must be a real doozy! What is going on? I guess I'm just being lazy. That's why I don't want to talk. I should stop being such a snob and talk to these people. I'm still confused by the word rehabilitation. In a few days maybe Dr. Lee, some of the other patients, and I can sit Indian-style on the floor and discuss this. Does rehabilitation mean sitting around and talking?

EIGHT

Visitors

That evening the sister of an old boyfriend visited me. She said, "Hi, Laura."

Now who is this? I recognize your voice, but I can't tell who you are through the blurs. ... Oh! Hi, Gail! What are you doing here?

Gail continued cheerfully, "I came up to see you on my break."

That's right. You work here at Lutheran General Hospital. I could sort of make out her uniform through the blurs. . . . Then I remembered how I must have looked.

Gail, I don't want you to see me like this. I still don't feel like talking. Please, go away. It's really nice of you to come, but go away.

She said, "I brought you a basket of silk flowers."

I bet they're pretty, but please go away.

She continued, "I'll put them on your bed-side table."

What's her brother's name? My old boyfriend? I can't think of it right now.

Gail said, "My mom, dad, and Glen say hello. They all hope you'll feel better soon."

Glen! That's his name! Please, Gail, don't tell him what I look like. I feel like such a wreck! I'll pretend I'm sleeping. Then maybe you'll go away.

Soon I heard soft footsteps leaving the room, and I quickly opened my eyes.

I don't see anyone. She's gone! Nurse – nurse. Turn me over.

With this discomfort, it was not hard to cry. Soon I was screaming, and the nurses were there.

The next day two women came to my room. One of them came close and spoke, "My name is Ruth. I'll be your speech therapist." Pointing to the other woman in the room, she said, "This is my student. Her name is Tricia." Without a pause, Ruth began my therapy. In a harsh voice, she said, "Try to say Ah."

Recoiling at her tone, I froze like a child too scared to talk. Ruth waited for my response. I made a feeble attempt to speak, but I didn't make a sound.

I'm sick and tired of being unsuccessful at things that used to come so easily. Ruth, just go away! I don't feel like putting up with you or your speech therapy garbage!

Ruth pushed on in her unnerving tone, "Stick out your tongue."

I tried as hard as I could in order to show her how I felt about her. *I wish I could stick out my tongue really far. If I could, I would stick it out soooo far, like "Naaa – naaa ---- na–na -- naa!" That would really feel good!*

When I couldn't do that, Ruth arrogantly barked a few more commands, none of which I could do.

I'm tired of playing your games! Just leave me alone!

She demanded, "Close your eyes."

Not wanting to do it, I did close them just to shut her out of my sight. Feeling strange knowing that Ruth and Tricia's eyes were focused on me, I struggled to keep mine shut. I opened them to Ruth storming from the room in a huff, her student trailing behind.

Am I relieved she's gone! I hope she never comes back. Good riddance! Who does she think she is, ordering me like that? I can do all those things she wants me to do. I just don't want to. When I decide to talk, all of these people will be so surprised. Then they'll send me home.

Nine

Dream

Is the temperature going up in here? I'm hot! I'M SO HOT! I'm glad Ruth left because I'm hot enough without her. She was making me angry. If only I could go home. I deserve to... my homecoming would be wonderful! I'd be on a float in a parade, wearing a beautiful pink gown like a fairy princess, my arms sheathed with long, white gloves, and I'd be waving a pink flowing scarf. There would be crowds of people clapping and shouting, "Good luck, Laura." I'd be waving my scarf saying, "Thank you – thank you."

Ruth would be at the head of the crowd shouting, "Oh, Laura, I'm so sorry. I didn't know you could talk, but you can! Yay, Laura!"

I'd say, "Goodbye, Ruth," waving her away. Then she and the other people at the hospital would all feel so ridiculous.

But in the meantime, I'm so hot. Would someone, please, turn off the heat?

Just then a nurse came in. *Please, nurse, don't go away. Help me. Stay with me.*

The nurse began moving me, turning and twisting me like a piece of licorice.

Hey, what are you doing? Stop that! You can leave now. I want to be left alone!

I could hear a man's voice. *He's talking to that nurse. What is he saying? . . .Ohhhh. . . I'm so hot. Whatever you're doing – stop. Wait! This nurse won't leave me alone.*

The nurse ordered in a bossy tone, "Laura, lie still. We can't get a specimen if you don't lie still."

That smell. What is that smell? Where have I smelled that odor before?

I'm back working at Dr. Zand's animal hospital. I have to hold onto an uncooperative dog so he doesn't get away. The doctor takes his right paw, but the dog squirms aside. I say, "Oh, no you don't, doggie. I'm smarter than you."

I get a firmer wrestling hold on the dog with my left arm, and my right hand holds onto the dog's paw for Dr. Zand who says, "Okay, Laura, let's try again." Using a cotton ball soaked in alcohol, he gently prepares the paw for a sodium pentathol injection.

Is that smell alcohol? Am I in the Twilight Zone? What is going on? My thoughts are back in my hospital room. *Yes, that smell is alcohol. What is that nurse doing to me? There is a man here that I think is a doctor. ... I'm so hot! ... Why am I here? Am I a dog? I don't know. All I know is that I have to get out of here.*

The nurse strains, "LAURA, HOLD STILL."

Okay, okay. I guess you're serious. I'll try to hold still.

"LAURA," she emphasized, her patience running low, "if you don't hold still, we'll have to strap you down so the doctor can get a specimen."

A specimen? A specimen of what? What are you doing to me? You're doing something to my back. I think I'm on my stomach on the floor like a snake. While the nurse was trying to hold onto me, I could hear the doctor moving up close. I could tell he had a needle because I know that "pop" sound of a needle cap coming off. My body kept slithering away, but I couldn't help it.

Again the nurse demanded, "LAURA. The doctor needs to get a specimen FOR YOUR OWN GOOD."

Can't you see I'm trying to hold still? If I am in the Twilight Zone, why can't you read my mind?

The doctor finally got his specimen, left, and the nurse kindly said, "Very good, Laura. I know it's hard for you to hold still because of your muscle spasms. You can rest now."

TEN

Shower

Two days later a nurse came in pushing a gurney. She said, "Laura, your fever is gone; your bladder infection is under control. I'll have to take these cones off your hands before I give you a shower."

A fever? Is that why I was so hot? What cones is she talking about?

She answered my inaudible question, "Cones look like cardboard tee pees that fit into the palms of your hands with Velcro straps that fasten around them."

I don't feel anything on my hands.

"They are to try to keep your fingers and hands relaxed." She took them off and asked, "You ready for your shower?"

I blinked twice for yes.

She pointed to a gurney, "This is a shower table."

There isn't anything special about that. How are you going to give me a shower on that thing?

She raised my bed, slid me over onto the table, and wheeled me out of the room. Now my hearing became acute; I recognized the buzz of the portable x-ray machine rolling down the hall, the clanking of the cafeteria trays in the tray holder, and the hub-bub of nurses and doctors shouting messages.

The nurse wheeled me into a room where I heard water running. The sound was getting closer, but I still couldn't focus. She said, "Here comes the water."

It feels so good!

When I was a teenager, one of my good friends moved to a small town in Missouri. I went to visit her for a couple of weeks during the summer. She had many cats, dogs, and other animals that I loved, but the most exceptional animal was a horse named Dolly. Sometimes, when it was hot, we would spray her with a hose. SHE LOVED IT! She would arch her back and hold her head up high.

Now in the shower room, the warm water mixed with the good smells of the soap and shampoo made me luxuriate in the feeling of getting clean. Soon the nurse dried me off, put a blanket over me, and pushed me on the shower table back to my room. The day I got that first shower, I felt like Dolly.

So that's how they give a shower here. Now I feel relaxed and sleepy.

ELEVEN

Is It Me?

When I woke up, Muriel, my roommate, was getting dressed and talking to a nurse.

Is she old? She sounds like it. I wish I could talk. I feel so dumb watching her, but there isn't anything else to do. I could watch TV, but I don't have my glasses on. The blurry vision has changed to a halo around objects. Between that and being near-sighted, I can't even see the images on the screen. I'll just pretend I'm watching TV.

Linda, a nurse, said to Muriel, who was sitting in her wheelchair, "Okay, Muriel. Now try to get your own bra on," as she handed the brassiere to her and walked out of the room.

There was Muriel, sitting like a lost puppy. Because I couldn't see well, I wasn't sure if she even tried to fasten her bra.

She swore and exclaimed, "I can't do this."

You can't do what? What is wrong with you?

Muriel was mumbling and grumbling like a little kid, calling out, "Linda, Linda, I need help."

What do you need help for? Can't you do something as simple as putting on your own bra? What a baby!

Linda came back and asked Muriel, "How are you doing?"

"Terrible. I can't get my bra fastened."

"Okay, I'll hook your bra for you, but tomorrow you can try

again. I want you to get some practice on buttons. I'll help you put your blouse on, but you try the buttons." She scurried out of the room, looked at me and said, "Sometime soon, you'll have to do this, too."

Oh, no, I won't! Not in a million years, and I won't whine like Muriel. I'll be fine as soon as someone gets me out of this bed. I hate it on this slab! I'm sick of it!

Muriel said, "These buttons are so small. I hate them! I'm going to have Ed bring me blouses with bigger ones."

What are you whining about? Just do the buttons on your shirt. Stop making such a big deal about it.

Soon Linda came back, "How's it going, Muriel?"

"Not very good. I got one button," said Muriel.

One button? That's all? I can't imagine what you were doing all this time! You're really lazy!

Linda said, "I'll do the rest of your buttons so you won't be late for therapy."

"Yes," said Muriel sarcastically, "I wouldn't want to be late for that."

I'll go for you. Anything – just get me out of this stinking bed! This is boredom city!

Muriel was off to therapy, and there I was lying on the bed with nothing to do. I couldn't even change my position in bed. Only being able to listen to the TV, I hoped that some nurses would come in so I could at least listen to them.

Nurses did come in, made Muriel's bed, and left.

Then I was all alone again. I decided to try to raise my right arm. With much straining, I could just barely see the old burn scar on my hand. *I remember that scar. I burnt it on the oven when I was 16 making chocolate chip cookies in Mom's kitchen. Then this must mean that the person in this bed is really me! How could it be me? Am I dreaming that this is happening to someone else? Oh. No. Oh, my! It IS me. IT'S REALLY ME! It can't be. Is this a nightmare? This isn't really happening, is it? No. It has to be a dream. I did have a migraine, but how long ago? I don't know. Migraines don't cause all of this. Do they? I don't think so. I've never heard of someone being put in the hospital for a simple migraine headache. I can't think of all this right now. I'm going to sleep.*

In a little while I woke up. As I raised my right arm again, I could see the scar on my hand. My arm dropped, out of control.

It's really true. I am the same person who burned her hand in the oven. And now, I am in the hospital. Could I still be having a nightmare?

Twelve

For Sure – It's Me!

Reality began to dawn on me that I couldn't do anything for myself at all. The hope I had that all of this was a nightmare started to dwindle. With this discovery came an irritating feeling in my right foot. It felt like my big toe was sticking out of a hole in my sock. Trying to wiggle my toe free, I couldn't loosen the grip my sock had on my big toe.

Marilyn came in asking, "Is there anything that you need?"

Oh, good. You can fix my sock. My head and shoulders still felt like a block of cement, so I blinked excitedly for yes.

She asked, "Do you want to lie in a different position?"

I blinked for no.

"Do you want the channel changed on the TV?"

I blinked for no.

"Do you want the light on?"

No again.

"Laura, I don't know what you want." She paused as she glanced around the room, "Oh, let me see. Do you want the TV off?"

I blinked for no. *Marilyn, please, my sock. Is my toe sticking out of a hole? Look at my foot. Look down there. Track my gaze! I'm directing you with my eyes!*

"Laura, I'm sorry. I don't know what you want. I'll come back. Maybe I can figure it out then."

Wait – Marilyn – wait!

Marilyn probed me with her eyes as she tried to study my thoughts, "What is it? I just don't know. I'm sorry."

Oh, it's no use!

As she left the room, I began to cry. *Why can't I do anything by myself? What's wrong with me?* Hoping to blot out the whole hospital scene, I closed my eyes as I cried hysterically.

Soon I heard some rustling about. Opening my eyes, I saw Mom in the doorway, and I stopped crying immediately as she walked in.

Having heard me cry, she asked, "What's wrong?"

I don't feel like talking to anyone right now. Talk – ha. I can't talk. Just go away, Mom. I want to be left alone.

She asked, "Is there anything I can do?"

I did not react.

Mom asked again, as I glared at her.

I don't feel like blinking. Leave me alone!

Just then a nurse came in asking, "Laura, is there anything you need?"

Leave me alone! Scowling at her with the same tormented eyes, I was beyond ordinary frustration. *I want to be able to talk, and tell people what I want. I want to be able to move around, and do what I want, when I want. Is there anything wrong with that? Oh, what is wrong with me? Nobody has told me! Did I have a migraine? Why couldn't it have happened to someone else?*

Mom asked the nurse, "Do you know what's wrong with Laura today? She isn't herself."

The nurse replied, "No, I don't know. Mrs. Klehr."

"Oh, please. Call me Carol," said Mom.

"Maybe she's tired, Carol."

"Honey," Mom asked like I was a little kid, "are you tired?"

Wanting to crawl into a hole and shut the whole world out, I closed my eyes, pretending to go to sleep.

The nurse asked, "Would you like something to drink, Carol? 7-Up?"

My eyes popped open. *7-Up? Maybe I'd like some 7-Up.*

Mom replied, "Yes, that would be nice."

Why doesn't she ask me? I'm not thirsty, but she should ask me just the same, I WANT SOME 7-UP! SHE ASKS MOM, BUT SHE DOESN'T ASK ME! WHAT KIND OF A HOSPITAL IS THIS?

Seeing something in my eyes, Mom inquired, "Laura, you're tired. Aren't you?

I didn't even blink.

She went on, "One of your neighbors sent you a card. Wasn't that nice? Do you want me to read it to you?"

Again, I didn't blink. *Leave me alone!*

Not getting a response from me, Mom cajoled me in her motherly tone, "You're tired, Hon. Why don't you close your eyes?"

I blinked twice for yes and closed my eyes. *Maybe now she'll stop bothering me.*

She said, "Take a nap. I'll read to you," and she read the card.

Then she opened a book and began reading it. Her voice hummed on and on, giving me comfort and bringing back memories of when I was a young child on Mom's lap while she read aloud. I didn't have a worry in the world then. Feeling drowsy, I soon fell asleep.

When I woke up, Mom was still sitting by my bed watching TV. Noticing I was awake, she scooted up to the end of her chair saying, "Oh, you're awake. Were you *ever* tired! You slept almost three hours. It's about time for me to go."

Mom, please don't go. Read to me some more. When you read, I forget all that's going on.

"Before I go," she continued, "the nurses suggested to me that I have you look in a mirror. I brought this mirror along." She held up a hand mirror to my face. "Can you see yourself?" she asked as she adjusted it.

For sure, it's me!

She said, "You haven't changed a bit. You're still Laura."

I look so sad!

THIRTEEN

Occupational Therapy (O.T.)

Soon Mike came and Mom left.

Oh, Mike. I'm so glad to see you! You wouldn't believe the kind of day I've had so far.

Mike chuckled, "I'm a little late because our dogs got into mischief. Megan is really into chewing everything and anything she can find, and Scraps sees Megan getting attention for that, so he chews up Kleenex. Scraps chewed up a whole box, ripped every sheet to shreds, and dragged it all over the house."

That's right. We have two dogs. I remember now. Megan is a puppy and Scraps is two years old. I started laughing, forgetting, for a short time, all my cares.

Then out of the clear blue Mike asked, "How's your memory?"

Unconsciously, I blinked for yes, meaning fine. Then I thought about the question. *Why is he asking me that? Of course, my memory is fine.*

He nodded in agreement saying, "I thought so, but the doctors said it could be affected."

Because I couldn't move or get out of bed, I felt imprisoned within myself. *I feel like I'm strapped down, but there are no ties holding me. I'm a caterpillar in a cocoon! I'm stuck in this bed! ...WHAT IS WRONG WITH ME?*

When no one was visiting me, I would sleep because I was bored. This made sleeping at night extremely difficult. Usually, I would lie awake.

There was an overnight nurse who would come and talk to me. On some nights she would talk to me for hours about God. I appreciated hearing the sound of her voice. It was a good reminder that I was still a part of the human race. However, the God-topic was totally unimportant to me. I didn't reflect on her words or remember them.

Some days, I could see fairly clearly, and other days not. Some days. I could nod and shake my head; however, other days I couldn't, and I had to regress to blinking.

Because I was bedridden, the therapists would come to me. A therapist came in the room one day. She greeted me and introduced herself.

"Hi, Laura. My name is Carol. I'm your occupational therapist. Occupational therapy helps you with activities of daily living, and with using your upper extremities. O.T. stands for occupational therapy. S.T. stands for speech therapy, and P.T. stands for physical therapy. Have you met your physical therapist yet?"

I shook my head no.

She said, "Oh, you will. I think you have Diane. You'll like her. She's really nice."

Taking hold of my right arm, Carol said, "Right now, I'll mainly work with your arms. I'll do some passive exercises with you. That means that I'll do the exercises for you," she explained as she began bending and straightening my arm. Soon she said, "Laura, let me see you move your right arm."

Concentrating on lifting my arm off the bed, I raised it about two feet. When I got it up high, she said, "Very good."

With that, I let it fall to the bed. Seeing her surprised expression, I started laughing in that spasmodic way that was becoming so familiar to me now.

She said while smiling, "No, no, no. You should let it down slowly. Control it. Let's try that again."

I lifted it as high as I could, and then I let it down slowly.

"Yes, that's much better. You know you can practice that. Make sure that you rest quite a long time between trials. Resting is very important."

Going around to the other side of the bed, she said, "Your right arm is loose, but your left arm is like a vice grip. Does it hurt?" she asked as she tried to pry it free of the grasp it had on itself.

I semi-nodded my head. My left arm was bent tight, elbow cramped against my chest, wrist bent sharply, fingers tightly clenched in a steel embrace.

As she tried to straighten my arm out, she watched my eyes as they bulged a little in pain. Carol put my arm down gently and touched me on the shoulder saying, "I'll be back tomorrow. See you then."

FOURTEEN

Frankenstein

The following morning, two women came in, and one woman, smiling cheerfully said, "Hi, Laura. How are you?"

Who are you? I don't recognize your voice.

"Let's see, last time you weren't able to stick out your tongue. Can you do it today?"

Last time? What's she talking about? I've never seen or heard her before. I tried sticking my tongue out, but again I was unsuccessful.

She said, "That's okay. You can try again tomorrow." She smiled at me with understanding.

I can see pretty well today, and she doesn't look like anyone I have halfway seen before. Could this person be Ruth, the speech therapist who was nasty to me? . . . NO!

She went on, still smiling, "Why don't you try to say, *AH*. Give it a good try."

I did just that, but not the slightest hint of a whisper passed my lips.

She said, "Okay, try again, but this time take in as deep a breath as you can. As you exhale, let out an *Ah*." She took in a deep breath and demonstrated.

Trying to imitate her, my body just wouldn't cooperate with

my will. *Could this be Ruth? It doesn't sound like her. This lady sounds much nicer, and she even has a smile.*

She said, "That's enough therapy for now. You look really tired. Oh, here's my notebook," she mentioned as she picked something up off my bedside table. "I must have left it when I was here yesterday. See you tomorrow."

It has to be Ruth. She must have had a bad day when she was here before. After that, I closed my eyes and fell asleep.

Soon I was being nudged by a woman saying, "Laura, wake up, wake up. My name is Diane, and I'm going to be your physical therapist." She walked around the bed to my legs as she said, "I'll work mainly with your legs. In physical therapy, or P.T. We are chiefly interested in getting you to walk again."

I bet I can walk. Just get me out of this bed, and I'll show you.

Diane began lifting and bending my legs. Soon she was working on my left arm.

Please, Diane, leave that arm alone. It really hurts when you move it.

She said, "The more we try to straighten out this arm, the less likely a contracture will develop. A contracture is when the muscles get so tight that a joint can no longer move."

I was dreading the pain yet to come. She had to put her bodyweight into pulling my arm back. As she barely moved it away from my chest, my eyes bulged with excruciating pain. *I know it now! I am Frankenstein, the monster! Diane is trying to yank on my limbs. The nurses are all mad scientists, fiddling with the bottles that dangle over me on the IV hanger. They are mixing their potions in these bottles, trying to squirt life into my lifeless flesh. I wish my eyeballs had electricity. I'd zap Diane to let her know I've had enough.*

Diane stopped and held my arm still for a few seconds. When she released it, I felt instant relief. She let out an exhausted puff of air as she said, "Pretty soon we'll get you on the tilt table."

She explained to me what it was, but I didn't listen to her. My idea of a tilt table was much more exciting. *Maybe the tilt table is like a game where you sit in the center of a table, and it tilts like a teeter totter. There are alligators swimming underneath in a swamp, and if you get too close to the edge, you could fall in the swamp. If you fall in, it will be lunchtime for the alligators.*

Soon Diane left and before I knew it, she was back wheeling in a gurney, saying, "Laura, this is a tilt table."

It isn't like anything I imagined. It's just a regular gurney.

She had a couple nurses help her get me onto the tilt table and strap me in. Then she wheeled me into the physical therapy room. She turned on a motor underneath the table in the place where the swamp filled with alligators should be.

Nothing's happening! Aren't I supposed to be quickly tilting like some amazing ride at the amusement park, like a tilt-o-whirl? I don't feel any tilting at all.

She said, "Okay, Laura. You'll stay like that for fifteen minutes."

I'll stay like what? You didn't do anything! What's going on?

She came back asking, "Do you feel dizzy?"

I blinked once for no. *Dizzy? I don't feel dizzy. Why should I?*

Then Diane explained again about the tilt table by saying, "Its function is to get you used to being in a vertical position, straight up and down. You've been in bed quite a while. The tilt table gradually tips you until eventually you're vertical. Sometimes patients get dizzy, but you don't seem to be. When you can withstand it to be straight up and down, the nurses will put you in a wheelchair. Now I'll get you horizontal and take you back to your room."

Diane came with the tilt table a few more times, and soon I was in a vertical position. My mind swirled with thoughts. *I expect she'll undo the straps one day soon, and I'll stomp away in a monster-like trance. My arms will poke out straight in front of my body; my legs and feet will move in a slow, zombie-like tread, just like Frankenstein, the monster!*

FIFTEEN

Raggedy Ann, Meet Your Wheelchair

If I listened real hard, I could hear nurses and doctors chattering out in the hall. There was talk of getting me out of bed.

Oh, I hope so. I'm so tired of lying in this bed. I want to get up and see what rehabilitation is like. The problem is that I can't get out of bed, and I can't move my legs at all. That sock is bothering me again! Maybe Dr. Frankenstein's assistant, Dr. Lee, is using some kind of torture method on me.

After lying in bed for what seemed like eons, I felt anticipation when three nurses filed in. The anxious feeling in my knees escalated into excitement as they came over to my bed and the nurse in front spoke, "Laura, we're going to get you out of bed."

Yahoo! Hip ...hip ... hooray! Finally, I'll get off this slab!

Mike and Mom were there again, and they watched as the trio of nurses hoisted my body like a side of beef into the wheelchair. The wheelchair supported my head so I was able to lean backwards. Mike held the palm of his hand out in front of my forehead a few inches away saying, "On the count of 3, push your head forward, but try not to let it flop. Ready? ... 1 ... 2 ... 3."

My head would go smashing into his hand with no control at all. I was a clone of Raggedy Ann, my neck a swatch of limp fabric. He continued the exercise, and I persevered trying to control my neck muscles. He would give me a rest between trials.

After a few times, Mike said, “Okay that’s enough for today,” and put his hand down by his side. “We’ll practice again tomorrow.”

I rested my head against the headrest, but wanting to continue, I soon pushed my head forward again. Mike was totally taken by surprise! He caught my head, exclaiming, “Whew, that was close! I guess you didn’t think it was enough.”

Mom said prudently, “Okay, honey, now rest.”

Cautiously, Mike kept his hand out in front of my forehead. I did take a break because Mom suggested it, but I was soon back to strengthening my neck muscles. This went on for as long as I could endure sitting up.

Please, I want to be put back to bed NOW. I’ve never felt so exhausted in my life, not running on the high school track team, not ever! It came on me so fast.

As much as I had wanted to be put in a wheelchair, now I wanted even more to go back to bed. Mike, seeing my weariness, asked, “Laura, do you want to go back to bed?”

Blinking an exhausted yes, *I’m going to die!*

He told one of the nurses, who then came over asking, “Laura, can you stay up five minutes longer?”

I’m exhausted! In fact, I’m past exhausted. I’m almost dead!

Barely blinking in response to her question, I managed two faint blinks for yes, but I felt like I wasn’t going to be alive much longer.

She answered, “Good. I promise in exactly five minutes, I’ll get two other nurses to help me put you back to bed.” My arms, legs, neck, and buttocks all ached, but no matter how hard I tried, I wasn’t able to sleep sitting up. The five minutes seemed like five hours. Finally the trio of nurses came to hoist me back into bed.

Ah! This feels so good!

After a short while, my anxiety about being back in bed returned along with the feeling of that annoying hole in my sock.

I'll try to shut them out. Tomorrow I'll practice in the wheelchair again.

Many tomorrows came and went for Raggedy-Ann-Laura, and soon my neck was strong enough to hold my head up. I could nod or shake my head almost all the time in response to questions, but I still had the wheelchair with the neck support for times when I was too tired to hold my head up.

So here I am in my wheelchair. Now what? I'm ready for anything.

Seeing other patients propelling their own wheelchairs made me think, *I can do that, too.*

Being able to only move my right arm a little bit, I could barely curl my fingers around the push wheel, moving the chair about one inch with each try. I soon realized that I was going around in circles. If I didn't want that, my right leg had to help. My left leg was on a foot rest, so I had only my right to work with.

A nurse came to help me. She instructed, "Try to stretch your right leg out in front of you, dig your heel into the floor, and pull your leg toward you to cause the wheelchair to move."

Coordinating my arm with my leg was some tricky business, but I eventually got the hang of it after many, many trials and errors. Now I would move about four inches instead of one. I knew I was no speed demon. The other patients would whiz by in their wheelchairs, and many of them would be using only one arm and one leg. If I wanted to catch up with them, I knew I had my work cut out for me.

WOW! How do they go so fast? I sure wish I could do that! I am going to do it! I AM!

Sixteen

Locked-in Syndrome

About six weeks into my hospitalization, Mike and Mom were visiting again. We were in my room, and I heard them discussing something. Only half-listening, I caught a startling phrase as Mom casually said, "....because Laura had a stroke."

Those words caught my attention. *What? I had a stroke? NO! Only old people have strokes! How could I have had a stroke? Exactly what is a stroke? Why didn't they tell me? Did they tell me?*

Now I was really alert to what Mom might say. She continued, "Dr. Lee says they call it the locked-in syndrome because Laura is trapped within her body with no way to express herself. She is like a prisoner within her own body!"

Yeah. Yeah, she's right. I want to be able to tell someone how mad I am this happened to me. Why me? What did I ever do to deserve this?

The locked-in syndrome is a condition in which the person is aware but cannot communicate verbally due to complete paralysis of nearly all the voluntary muscles in the body except for the eyes.

Mom continued, "Not one doctor will say why she had the stroke. They say it must have been a fluke."

A fluke? Why don't the doctors know?

Soon a nurse came in with a device. She said, "Laura, this is a special call button. It's real easy to squeeze because it's made of soft rubber. Why don't you try it?" she encouraged as she placed it in my hand.

I tried it once, twice, and on the third time I was able to squeeze it, although it wasn't enough to turn on the light.

The nurse said, "Try again."

Finally, I was successful. The light lit, and immediately I started laughing.

Seventeen

The Talking Eyes

The days went by slowly. I had no idea how long I would be stuck at Lutheran General Hospital.

I surely won't be here very long at all. Probably I'll be home in a week!

Sometimes the stroke seemed factual, sometimes just fantasy. Events surrounding me were often somber, but sometimes funny.

One evening Sam, my brother-in law, came in and told Mike, Mom, and me a true story. It happened that evening when he came and pulled into the front parking lot of the hospital. He saw a sign that read *Rehabilitation*. He thought to himself, *This is the place.*

He went to the unit's front desk and asked the nurse, "Where is Laura Barnett's room?"

The nurse looked at her log, "How do you spell her last name?"

"B-A-R-N-E-T-T."

She looked for a few minutes longer and then asked him, "How do you spell that last name again?"

Sam, in a relaxed way, spelled my name for her once more. She looked through each individual chart, but she was unable to find the room. By now, Sam was getting irritated. Finally the nurse asked him, "Does she drink?"

Sam thought this was a strange question. He replied, "Oh, I guess she has a few."

A little annoyed, the nurse retorted, "This is ALCOHOL rehabilitation. You want PHYSICAL rehabilitation. It's in the other building on the sixth floor."

We all just laughed and laughed.

One Saturday a nurse came in and woke me saying, "Your husband is here with his sister, brother-in-law, and their two kids. I'll get you dressed and into the wheelchair. You can go in the lounge and visit."

I don't want to see the kids again. They were here the other day. When they came, all I could do was cry. I think I scared them.

Mike came in. "Good morning, sleepy-head," he said cheerfully. "It's almost 10:00 am. Are you going to sleep the day away?"

Teasing him back, I nodded.

"I'll wait in the hallway while the nurse gets you dressed."

Soon the nurse handed me off to Mike, and he pushed me down the hall toward the lounge saying, "Try not to cry because the kids get really scared."

Easier said than done, but I'll try.

We went into the lounge and found all four of them, Sam and Phyllis with a child on each lap. Tony was three and Christina was six months. "Hi, Laura," Sam and Phyllis said in unison. Then Phyllis said, "Tony and Christina really miss their aunt. Right guys?" The children were preoccupied with their new surroundings, not paying the slightest attention to me.

I can't even see them clearly. Why won't this blurry vision go away? Oh, no! I think I'm going to cry!

Noticing my expression, Phyllis quickly asked with a mischievous smile, "Laura, is my brother treating you okay?"

I nodded my head, and Mike, his voice full of sarcasm,

interrupted, "No, I keep her in a dark room with no visitors. You're her first visitors."

"I thought so," Phyllis said with a conspiratorial smile.

Sam added, "Isn't it like a brother and sister to fight?"

Phyllis asked, "Laura, have you been in any wheelchair races yet?"

Laughing, I shook my head no.

Sam smiled and said, "Why not? Before you know it, you'll be racing up and down these halls."

During this exchange, three-year-old Tony was busy swiping a cane from one of the patients nearby. Noticing this, I laughed my fog horn laugh which startled both Christina and Tony. Tony had been heading behind a chair with the patient's cane, but when I laughed, he stopped abruptly. Phyllis spied Tony with the cane and rushed over to him. The patient was gentle and, fortunately, in good humor. He laughed, "I need the cane to walk, little guy."

Within a few minutes, everyone went back to talking while Tony was once again plopped on Phyllis's lap. Trying to confine Tony was very difficult. Phyllis finally gave in to his relentless wiggling. She put him down and soon Tony had the patient's cane again.

Tony began to walk away with the cane while the patient was immersed in a conversation. No one seemed to notice Tony, except me, despite my double vision. I kept looking at Mike to get his attention, and finally he glanced at me. Motioning with my eyes, I followed Tony as he was getting closer to the door. Mike hopped up, grabbed Tony, and returned the cane.

When he sat down he said, "You know, Laura was the only one who saw Tony swipe the cane and run., and she communicated that to me with her eyes. Laura can talk with her eyes!"

Phyllis chimed in, "Yeah, Mike, so can I. What are my eyes saying?" She gave him a nasty look.

We all started laughing, and soon our visit was over. On the way back to my room, Mike said, "Congratulations. You didn't cry."

I nodded my head in satisfaction. *That's right! I didn't!*

Eighteen

Whoever Called It a Rest-Room?

I don't remember when Muriel left and Charlotte arrived. Charlotte was my new roommate. Because of her, I began to understand how specific a stroke can be. Soon I would learn that stroke affects each person differently. Charlotte, for instance, had only a slight weakness on her right side and needed just a cane. In contrast, I was in a wheelchair with both sides paralyzed, yet, my right side was coming back. We were very different.

Charlotte and I were similar in one way, though. We both had a serious communication problem. I could not talk, and Charlotte had *aphasia*. For her, that meant that she had trouble getting words out. She told me words were on the tip of her tongue, but it was difficult for her to say them. Sometimes she would succeed after two or three tries; other times, she would just give up in frustration. Each day Charlotte and I worked hard toward normalcy in communication through speech therapy.

With my continued progress, I was now capable of using my call button easily. However, the double vision wouldn't go away. It was erratic and, therefore, unnerving. Some days my vision would be good, and other days it would be miserable.

Will it ever go away?

One morning Mary Joy, one of the nurses, wheeled in a strange contraption, saying, "This is a shower chair."

A shower chair? Today my vision is pretty good. It looks like a wheelchair toilet, but it's empty underneath. It's also on wheels.

Mary Joy said to Charlotte, "You can go take a shower by yourself."

Charlotte stammered, "W ...wh...which...one...sh...sh... should...I...u...us...use?"

"The one at the end of the hall."

Charlotte nodded and left.

Mary Joy got another nurse and transferred me to the shower chair. She wrapped a blanket around me and wheeled me down the hallway into a large shower room.

Why can't I take a shower by myself? I wish I was like Charlotte.

Mary Joy hosed me off with an extended shower head. She did all the work, but I didn't mind.

It feels so good to get clean!

She dried me off, wrapped a blanket around me, and wheeled me back to my room. There, a nurse helped her put me back into bed. Mary Joy began dressing me by first putting long, white stockings on me. "These are support hose." she said, "They help your circulation."

So, I AM wearing socks! These socks go all the way past my knees. I wonder if they have a hole by the toe.

Mary Joy said, "See?" as she held them up for me to look at.

They do have a hole in the foot! It's like she's putting nylons on me, but they're awfully tight!

These socks were compression hose so my legs would not swell. The hole exposes the toes allowing for nail trimming without removal of the hose.

Then Dr. Lee came in saying, "Hi, Laura."

She and Mary Joy started discussing whether or not I was ready to have the catheter removed from my bladder. If they took it out, I would have to relearn when I needed to use the rest room.

Mary Joy asked the doctor, "Do you think she's ready?"

I'm ready! I'm ready!

Mary Joy questioned Dr. Lee, "How will we know when she has to go to the bathroom?"

Dr. Lee said, "Well, she can push the call button."

Directing the next question to me, she asked, "Laura, can you point your finger?"

I slowly and methodically bent my three outer fingers and my thumb inward, pointing with my index finger, though it would not straighten completely. Still, Dr. Lee and Mary Joy exclaimed, "You did it!"

That sense of accomplishment started me laughing and they just smiled. Mary Joy patted me on the shoulder as Dr. Lee said to her, "She's ready."

Yes! Thank you, Dr. Lee!

Mary Joy said, "Okay, Laura. If you have to go to the bathroom and you're near your call button, press it. When a nurse comes in, point your finger. If you're not near your call button, cry, and again point your finger when the nurse comes. That will be our special code."

Then she continued getting me dressed with a pair of white pants. She said, "These are the hospital's pants. You'll wear them for a while until you get better control of your bladder. Your husband brought in some of your shirts from home," and she held them up.

I remember those.

"I'll put one of these on you. How about this green one?"

Happy to have something from home, I nodded my head.

She and another nurse transferred me into the wheelchair and to the hall.

"Okay, you're on your own. Don't forget about our code."

Immediately, I started my inchworm movement in the wheelchair. It seemed like it took forever for me to go about ten feet, but if I wanted to go as fast as those other patients, I knew I had hard work ahead of me.

Suddenly I had to go to the bathroom. Trying to cry, I just couldn't make a sound.

Nurse. Nurse, I have to go. Come here and take me to the bathroom.

Because I was not able to cry to alert the nurses, I couldn't hold it any longer, and I went.

Oh, brother!!

Just then a nurse came over and noticed my wet pants. She asked, "Laura, did you have an accident?"

I nodded my head vigorously.

She and another nurse transferred me to my bed to change me, and afterward put me back in the wheelchair. One of them pushed me out into the hallway saying, "Go to it, Laura."

Though I stayed up in the wheelchair as long as I could bear it, I soon was ready to be put back to bed. Thinking about my discomfort, I was able to cry to get the nurse's attention.

She came over asking, "Laura, do you want to go back to bed?"

I nodded my head, but I couldn't stop crying.

She said, "Okay, let me get someone to help."

While I waited, *Why can't I stop crying? Why can't I stay up in the wheelchair all day? Why am I not more like those other patients? Why don't I have at least one good arm and leg? Why did I have this stroke, anyway? Oh, why? Why? Why?*

The nurses put me back to bed and went on with their business.

Soon Mom came in while I was still crying. "What's the matter, Honey?"

Not knowing what else to do, I pointed at my wheelchair.

"What's wrong with your wheelchair?"

Frustration pushed me into crying hysterically... *Oh, what's the use?*

"Were you in the wheelchair three hours?" Mom asked.

I shook my head no angrily.

"Two hours?" she asked.

I nodded my head yes.

"Laura, that's good. But you need to rest now. It's very important that you rest. Do you think you'll get better, if you don't?"

I nodded my head. *You bet! I want to get well NOW! I want to get up and walk right out of here. I want to tell them at the nurses' station that I don't need to be here anymore. Why did I have this stroke? Why me? Why couldn't it have been someone else? What did I do to deserve this?*

The next morning I woke up, and I had hopes that all of this was a nightmare. Soon my inability to move forced me into reality. *I know I had a stroke. But it's so unbelievable!*

Marilyn came into my room with the shower chair and said, "Laura, I'm going to give you a shower today."

I nodded my head.

We went into the shower and Marilyn began washing me. She said, "Oh, I forgot the shampoo. I'll be right back."

I'll just continue to wash myself.

With that, I bent over to wash my legs, and I toppled over onto the floor. I started screaming.

Marilyn rushed in and found me on the floor with my head bleeding. She got a couple of nurses to help put me back in the shower chair and back to bed. My head needed 4 stitches, and I had to stay in bed until the next morning.

A few days later, I was resting in bed and had to go to the

bathroom again. Because I was getting better at pushing my call button, I signaled a nurse with it.

Carolyn came in asking, "What can I do for you?"

I pointed my finger the best I could.

She said, "You used our code! Do you have to go to the bathroom? Can you hold it while I get another nurse to help me transfer you? I want you to start getting used to the toilet instead of using a bedpan.

I nodded my head enthusiastically for yes.

"I'll be right back," she said as she rushed out of the room.

Please, hurry! I'm afraid I'll have another accident.

Quickly she came back bringing another nurse with her. They lifted me into the wheelchair, pushed me into the bathroom, and heaved me onto the throne.

Even though I didn't weigh a lot, I could tell by the looks on their faces that this was hard work because I was dead weight. Once I was on the toilet, I felt like I was balancing on a high wire, teetering back and forth. Because of the paralysis of my left arm, I only had my half-paralyzed right arm to hold me up.

Thank goodness they have bars near this toilet, so at least I can hold on with my right hand.

Carolyn said, "We'll leave you here so you can have some privacy. There's a pull chain by your right hand for you to call the nurse. Can you pull it?"

Each time I tried to let go of the grab bar to reach for the chain, I fell over to the left and Carolyn, quickly catching me, said, "That won't work."

She had another idea. "What if I put the pull chain in your hand?"

She tried that and said, "Okay, try it now."

I tried, but not having enough strength in my hand to pull the chain and hold on at the same time, I again fell over to the left without the slightest tug on the chain.

Carolyn said, "I'll just come back in a few minutes."

I waited there thinking that I never imagined the "restroom" could be such hard work!

One day, Mike took me to a part of the hospital grounds with a nice patio and many benches. It had a flower garden filled with petunias. Mike picked a pink flower and put it in my hair. He always made me feel special!

Soon I had to go to the bathroom but didn't want to leave. Besides, Mike didn't know how to assist me in the bathroom and there was not one close. Lutheran General is a large hospital. We were on the first floor, but my room was on the sixth.

I'll be able to hold it. Before I knew it, I went. *Maybe Mike won't notice.*

In a few minutes Mike asked, "Should we head back now?"

I nodded yes. There was a ramp leading downward to the elevators. Mike made sure that no one was coming from the other direction as he rolled me down the slope and let go. Then he said, "Bye, Laura," as he lifted both of his hands in the air to let me know that I was traveling on my own. I acted surprised as if I was going to crash, but I knew Mike wouldn't let that happen. Soon he was running after me, and it seemed like he caught me just in time.

We took the elevator up to the sixth floor and went back to my room. He stayed with me a little while, and then he left.

The nurses cleaned me up and put me to bed.

I knew that being in the wheelchair, my only means of transportation until I was able to walk, and this was only temporary. Because I was getting accustomed to the wheelchair and adept at using it, I began having speech, occupational, and physical therapies in the specific departments, each twice a day. I enjoyed the activity of being up and about, and I was happy about the progress I was making.

Nineteen

Do You Get My Point?

I was in Ruth's office having speech therapy. She said, "Try to say, AH."

I tried, and a little sound came out, not a crying sound but an AH.

Ruth's eyes lit up as she exclaimed, "Way to go, Laura!" I started to laugh and couldn't stop. Ruth just smiled and giggled every now and then, patiently waiting for me to stop laughing.

When I settled down, she asked, "Laura, can you do that again?"

I tried again and again, but I wasn't able to make even the tiniest of sounds.

Over and over I tried until Ruth said, "That's okay. We'll try again this afternoon."

Why is AH so tough to say?

Everything was tough. Tough became a common word in my silent vocabulary, but with every success, I moved on to a new tough activity. There was no getting away from tough. Nothing was easy!

One day Diane, my physical therapist, took me in my wheelchair to her department. *What a busy place,* As we entered. *I didn't notice it when I was here on the tilt table.* There were many tables that were about knee-high, each covered with an exercise mat. *They look like double beds.*

We had to wait while a male patient walked through the aisle with a cane in one hand and a therapist holding his other arm. After they went by, Diane pushed me over to an unoccupied exercise area. Pointing to it, she said, "This is a mat table."

In the room, there were many mat tables and in the middle of the room was a set of practice stairs. *I'll be on the stairs next week. No problem. A few days after that, I'll be walking by myself at home.*

Diane had another therapist help her transfer me from the wheelchair to the mat table. After Diane got me situated on it by laying me on my back and bending my knees, she held my feet so they wouldn't slide. She said, "Okay, Laura. I want you to try to lift your bottom off the mat."

I tried, but again, as with everything else, I was unable to do it. Trying over and over, I didn't have any success.

Diane said, "Try to dig your feet into the mat."

Concentrating, I was able to lift my bottom a fraction of an inch off the mat. *Alright! I did it!*

Immediately, I started laughing out of sheer joy.

Diane said. "That's really good." She smiled as I continued laughing. "Now I think you should rest for a while." She put my legs down and began making small talk. My laughter stopped as I listened to her, and then she got up and said, "I'll be right back. You just lie here and rest."

There was a man sitting on the mat nearest me telling a patient in a wheelchair about the artificial leg he had with him. "This is a prosthesis. You have to be really careful when you wear it so your stump doesn't get sore." He pointed to a leg that wasn't there.

Oh, my! That person must have had his leg chopped off! I used to think that would be so awful! Now I would rather have that than this stroke!

Diane came back and continued my exercise session broken with long rest periods. Finally she said, "Okay, we'll do more tomorrow." Then she took me back to my room.

Even though I'm right-handed, I lacked enough strength or coordination to hold a pen or pencil. Ruth had mentioned in passing that she had an idea to help me communicate.

One day, I was in the wheelchair in the hall just watching the daily routine of the nurses. Ruth walked up to me holding a strange apparatus. She smiled and said excitedly, "This is a communication board. It has a sling to support your right arm! Here, let me show you."

She placed an alphabet board, which she said had been made by a friend of mine, across my lap. Then she tightened a crane-like device onto the arm of the wheelchair with a C-clamp. The crane had a strap dangling from it which she said was the sling.

It looks like an erector set that my brothers got for Christmas when we were little kids. How is this gadget going to help me communicate?

She placed my right arm in the sling, which was suspended over the communication board like an airplane buzzing above the airport waiting to land.

Ruth said, "Try to point your index finger."

Even though I was used to using pointing as a restroom signal, it was still a difficult maneuver. Finally, my index finger was ready for this new job. She adjusted the sling downward so I could just touch the letters on the board.

Then she asked, "Can you spell the word PEN?"

That doesn't sound too difficult. I studied the communication board, which looked like this:

COMMUNICATION BOARD

A B C D E F G H I
J K L M N O P Q R
S T U V W X Y Z ?
0 1 2 3 4 5 6 7 8 9

As I tried, my shoulder wanted my arm to hug my body closely; it didn't want to cooperate with my eager crooked index finger. Thinking specifically about moving my shoulder, I really had to concentrate. M*aybe it's a little harder than I thought. Come on, shoulder, just a little farther. There we go. Come on, a little bit farther. Come on . . . all right!*

It seemed to help if I talked to my body parts, even if I talked in my mind. Very slowly and painstakingly, I made it to the P, then to the E, and finally the N.

Ruth said, "Spell out the word MASK."

Noticing how far the letters were to the left, I glanced at Ruth, back at the board, and back at Ruth. *Well, what have I got to lose? Here goes!*

Taking a deep breath, I stretched toward the M and made it right away, but the A was so much further. Talking to my shoulder didn't work this time. I could only imagine my finger touching the letter. After trying at least three times, I pointed at the A. That was only half way. The S and the K were just as hard. But I did it! I spelled MASK!

Ruth exclaimed, "Way to go, Laura!"

Now with this new device, I could open for the world a peephole into myself. I was on my way to escaping the locked-in syndrome and had an intoxicating feeling about what was to happen next. With this communication board, even though it was not easy, I could tell people some of my thoughts and feelings.

What can I say to Ruth? You're nice? In a way, this will be like I'm meeting each member of the hospital staff for the first time! What do I say?

When a nurse came over to the wheelchair, I used the board to the best of my ability, I HAVE T0 GO TO THE BA –

She understood what I wanted and rushed me away to the bathroom, smiling.

Later that evening when Mike came in, I pointed the best I could to the letters of the communication board, HOW ARE YOU?

He was overjoyed. He answered, "I'm fine. How are you?"

Echoing him, I pointed to the letters F-I-N-E. *I don't know what to say to Mike. Instead of getting tongue-tied, I'm getting finger-tied.*

He asked, "Do you like the communication board?"

Feeling more elated than a child with a new toy, I pointed to the letters instead of nodding my head. Diligently, I spelled, YES.

Mike knew the answer even before he asked the question. We made small talk, but because pointing was so difficult, talk was never small.

Twenty

You Won't Believe What Happened In Group!

One day, Dr. Lee said, "Laura, I think you would benefit from group therapy."

I stared at her. *Group therapy? Isn't that for people who are insane?*

"It's an hour session," Dr. Lee continued, "where usually there are one or two group leaders and anywhere from five to ten patients. All the group members have had a stroke, brain damage from trauma, multiple sclerosis (MS), or an amputation. Usually they have a discussion. I think you will like it. Do you have any questions?"

I shook my head no. *I guess that's okay. I can't talk, so I won't be able to join in.*

In group therapy that day, a man and a woman led the group. There were six participants, all of us were in wheelchairs. The man said, "For those of you who don't know, I'm one of the chaplains of the hospital. My name is Chong."

He motioned to the woman sitting next to him, "And this is Carol, one of the social workers."

She nodded her head in greeting.

Chong went on, "Let's continue with our discussion where we left off yesterday." Sitting up straight in his chair he asked, "Now, do some of you feel you're going to be a burden to your children?"

Children? I've only been married a year! I don't have any kids yet! These people are all old! I don't belong here!

Chong went on, "Ralph, did you see your kids last night? What did. . . oh, I'm sorry. I forgot to introduce the newest member of our group."

Is he talking about me? As soon as he introduced me, it was like turning on a switch that opened a dam and sent the tears flowing. *I don't know why I'm crying, but I can't help it.*

Everyone knew who he was referring to because I was screaming louder than a blaring fog horn.

He continued, "Laura has had a stroke, and she has a communication problem."

By now, I was screaming so loudly that the chaplain had to shout. Even though I could only voluntarily make a soft grunting sound, when I involuntarily cried, it could be heard down the hallway.

I imagined him saying, "She can't talk, but she sure can cry." Oh, brother. I wish I could stop.

My crying went on and on. They tried to continue their discussion where they left off, but it was hard with me wailing unceasingly. Finally, Carol wheeled me out of the room and down to her office where she said, "Laura, I know it's hard for you. I think being in the group will really help you."

Crying so hard, I crammed my eyes shut. Before I opened them again, I thought, *maybe this is all a dream. When I look again, she'll be gone. I hope so.*

Carol said, "Come on, Laura. I'll take you back to your room."

My eyes opened a slit, and I saw her. *Oh, no! This isn't a dream! I wish all of you would just leave me alone!*

Carol took me back to my room where I continued to cry. She said, "See you tomorrow."

I have to do this again? ...maybe I'll hide.

Tomorrow came, and I was practicing going around the nurses' station in my wheelchair. Chong spotted me from across the hall. He raised his arm as he shouted, "Hi, Laura."

He caught my attention. *Oh, no. It's the man from Group. I guess it's too late to hide.*

He came over to talk to me, and I started sobbing. *Here I go again!*

He asked, "What's wrong?"

Realizing that many stroke patients do cry for no reason, he quickly changed the subject. "Oh, I brought you a large-print *Reader's Digest.*" I read on your chart that you have a little problem with your eyesight. This may help you see the words better."

Immediately, I stopped crying. *Oh good, maybe I CAN read it.*

He set it down on my communication board. Looking at the front cover, I was able to read a few words, but soon I felt like I was in a rocking ship on the ocean. The letters blended together.

He asked, "Are you able to read it?"

"NOT REALLY," I spelled on my board.

"Maybe in a little while you'll be able to," he said.

Then he asked, "How did you like Group yesterday?"

I began to cry. *Who turned on the water faucets again? Oh brother!* While still sobbing, I didn't want to get into it with him. *I hated it! I wish you would just leave me alone.*

"Laura, can you give me some words that describe your feelings about having a stroke?"

HATE!

Trying to point to the letters, I was screaming so hysterically that by now my eyes wouldn't open for me to see them. I was just moving my arm around at random.

He said, "I didn't catch that. Can you do it again?"

With that, I wailed as I thought, *HATE! HATE! HATE!*

"Laura, aren't you mad that this happened to you? Wouldn't you like to take it out on something? How about punching a pillow?"

Nodding my head yes, I was screaming again.

Chong went to get a pillow, which he laid across my communication board saying, "Give it a good punch."

Distracted, I stopped crying and tried to concentrate on pulling my arm back as far as I could. Aiming my fist at the pillow, I gave it the best wallop I could manage. THUD! It was a limp punch. *I don't feel like that helped. Aren't I supposed to feel relieved?*

Chong asked, "Do you feel any better?"

Shaking my head no, I tried again. *I still don't feel any better. Maybe if I could use both hands, one right after another, that might help. But my left arm won't move!* Resuming my crying, I tried punching the pillow repeatedly BAM-BAM-BAM, but I wasn't coordinated enough. All I could muster was a half hearted bump...-...bump. *Here I go again. I'm crying hysterically. Enough of this. LEAVE ME ALONE! I don't feel any better.*

Chong realized I'd had enough, so he put the pillow back and said, "Okay, Laura, I'll see you at 10:00. I'll come and get you when it's time for Group."

I have to go through this again? For sure, this time I'll hide in the bathroom. I'm glad he left. It will take me awhile to stop crying, but I will. Then I can get on with what I was doing before Chong was here. Practicing in my wheelchair, I was surprised when I looked at the clock and saw it was almost 10:00. *It's almost time for Group! I'll hide in the bathroom.* My mind tried to speed up my body, but I fumbled around and couldn't even turn the wheel. *Haste makes waste!*

I slowed myself down and inched into the bathroom. Managing to close the door halfway, I just sat there, exhausted. Pretty soon a knock was followed by a nurse opening it. She asked, "What are you doing in here?"

Oh, no! I'm caught!

I gave her an innocent look and a shrug, but I knew exactly WHY I was in there. Although she wasn't on to my tricks, she just said, "Well, I'll put you back in the hallway."

My clever escape is foiled, and I'm pooped! Now Chong will find me for sure.

Soon Chong came and took me to Group. I sat daydreaming as patients were brought in one by one, and I was startled when I heard my name.

"Laura," said Hank, a fellow patient whom I had met quite a few times before, "I see they corralled you in here."

I nodded my head yes.

Pointing to my communication board, he asked, "Well, what have we got here?"

Hearing the question, Chong replied, "It's her communication board. It allows her to say what's on her mind."

Hank maneuvered himself up to my wheelchair. Then he pointed on the board, "WHAT IS NEW?"

I pointed as best I could, "NOTHING."

"No," he said jokingly, "You're supposed to point to NEW Jersey or NEW Orleans."

He started laughing, but I didn't find anything funny in what he said. Not being able to courteously smile, I sat there with a frozen, stern look on my face.

He asked, "What's the matter?" He leaned over and said teasingly, "You should be smiling. The nurses don't give you prune juice." Distorting his face, he shuddered and said, "that stuff is awful!"

I laughed at his expression.

He turned to the others and cheered. "Alright! I got her to laugh!"

Many of the patients started laughing, too. Soon Chong and Carol had arranged us all in a circle.

Chong said, "Let's see ... Hank, Norm, Laura, and Adrian have had strokes; Annette is an amputee, and Louis and Charlie have MS. Now, everyone knows why everyone else is here."

We all looked around at each other.

"Yesterday," Chong continued, "we said that today would be sunshine day. We're going to brighten each others day. I'm going to ask you to say something nice about someone. Charlie, can you call Adrian a nice name that describes her personality?"

Charlie said, "Adrian gave me an apple yesterday. She is very generous."

Adrian laughed.

Chong said, "That's very good Charlie. Norm, what about you? What name can you think of for Annette?"

Norm stuttered, "Sh...sh...she...uh...uh...is...uh...kind."

Annette beamed.

Then Chong said, "Good. Laura, what do you think about ... ah ... Hank? What do you think he is?"

Concentrating on what to call Hank, I was so deep in thought that my crying was the last thing on my mind. Everyone's attention was directly on me, but it didn't bother me because I was concentrating extremely hard.

As I began pointing to my board, Hank followed my finger, saying the letters out loud,

"J – O – K – E – R. JOKER!"

Everyone started laughing.

Hank guffawed, "I don't believe it! She called me a JOKER!"

Soon everyone settled down and a new discussion began. I began to daydream again.

I'm deeply puzzled by the other stroke patients. Norm has a communication problem, and his right side is paralyzed. Hank has no communication problem, and his left side is paralyzed. What am I? I'm paralyzed on both sides with a big communication problem. What's going on? I must be different because I'm young.

Chong said, "Whenever you have a debilitating disease, such as stroke or MS, you must keep your mind active."

My mind is active.

He continued, "Crossword puzzles and other word games and puzzles all help to keep your brain functioning."

What's he talking about? I'm really confused!

Soon Group was over.

I feel much more comfortable. Now I don't mind coming here at all.

TWENTY-ONE

Laughter, the Best Medicine

One day my best girlfriend, Nancy came to visit while Mike was there. We had known each other since we were ten years old. We lived in the same neighborhood and went to high school together. We even worked together. At Eastern Illinois University we were roommates, and she was in my wedding.

In my hospital room she hollered, "Hi, Laura. How are you?" The sound battered my ears and echoed around the room.

Nancy, please! Don't shout again! Quickly nodding my head for fine, I braced myself as she nearly pierced my eardrums.

She bellowed, "Remember, Laura. I'm going to get married in April of 1981. You promised to be a bridesmaid in my wedding. It's only nine months away."

I nodded. *Yes, I remember now. Nancy you were in my wedding, and I'm going to be in yours. April is a long way off. I'll be well by then.*

She wanted affirmation as she asked loudly, "Okay?"

Vigorously, I nodded my head. *Yes Nancy, I know I will be well by then, but please, don't yell.*

Nancy shouted, "Anything good happening on our favorite soap opera?"

Mike broke in, "Nanc, you don't have to scream. She can hear okay. She just can't talk."

Nancy apologized, and we all laughed.

One day I was lying in bed taking a short rest from the day's activities. Marilyn came into my room holding this huge white brassiere. She was holding it away from her body as if it had a contagious disease. She sarcastically asked, "Laura, is this yours?"

Emphatically, I shook my head no.

She said, "It must be Muriel's bra. She forgot it when she went home."

Marilyn put the bra on over her uniform and put a couple of socks in the cups. It was still too big for her! Strutting about the room, she swayed her shoulders back and forth while holding her head up high like she was a fashion model wearing the latest style.

Sometimes when Marilyn and Carolyn came to work they would have funny stories about their two cats. Carolyn had Beau who kept himself very clean, and Marilyn had Maggie who was a slob. She would eat before Beau, lie around, and have him clean her.

One day they were both getting me dressed and ready for therapy. Marilyn said to Carolyn, "Hand me her shoes."

Carolyn teasingly said, "What if I don't want to. Not until you say, 'Please'."

Continuing the joking, Marilyn said, "No."

Carolyn taunted her, "Oh, yeah. Do you expect me to give you whatever you want just like Beau steps back and lets Maggie eat first?"

Marilyn firmly stated, "Well, Beau could eat first if he wanted."

"But he won't," Carolyn chided, "He's too much of a gentleman."

Marilyn said like a proud owner, "Maggie is a lady. She's very beautiful."

"She only got that way because Beau cleans her."

By this time I was laughing myself silly to hear them fake an argument. I still had the foghorn laugh and it truly sounded nerdy. It was times like these that made me feel like there wasn't anything wrong with me.

Smiling, Carolyn handed my shoes to Marilyn and said, "Just like Beau."

As I was going by the nurses' station one day, I saw a young man coming toward me in his wheelchair.

Oh, no! It's John R.!

The talk around the 6th floor was that he had been in a car accident and had suffered severe brain damage. The nurses had strapped him to his wheelchair so he wouldn't hurt himself. He swerved and banged into whatever was near him, without a care in the world. He looked right at people but didn't really see them. It was as if he were blind.

When I saw him coming, I stopped, more than a little anxious. John took off his t-shirt and the nurses commanded, "John! Put your t-shirt back on!"

There was no response from John as he continued his crooked course. After he got the t-shirt off, he took his pants off. There he was, sitting in the wheelchair, stark naked! All I could do was laugh. He continued on his weaving adventure until suddenly he crashed into a wall where his momentum was quickly brought to a halt.

His nurse looked up from her paperwork when she heard the crash. Seeing his nakedness, she shrieked, "JOHN!"

John straightened himself out and went back to crisscrossing the floor. Hearing my laughter at the "wheelchair centerfold" John's nurse burst out laughing. Snatching his clothes scattered down the hall, she grabbed him in his wheelchair and hustled him back to his room.

One Saturday, my roommate Charlotte was able to go out on a day pass for lunch with a friend. She came back from the restaurant smiling, fresh, a new person, stammering, "I…had …uh…filet… uh…uh…uh…mignon. Filet mignon!"

I haven't had that in a long time. I'm not hungry, but why is it that I can't eat? Hmm . . . I wonder.

Later, when Mom came to visit, she asked Charlotte, "How was your day pass?"

"Fine," she replied without hesitation, not one pause or gasp, not one "uh…uh…uh."

Knowing she had gone out to eat, Mom asked, "What did you have?"

She now attempted, "F…uh…f…uh…uh…fim…film…uh… uh…uh…filmo." She tried again, "Fim…uh…uh…uh…fimo… fim." And again, "Filmo mag…uh…uh…uh…folo migo…uh… uh…uh…falo migo…uh…uh…uh." She blurted out, "Ahhhh," while motioning her hand downward as if to give up. She was getting extremely frustrated.

Seeing that, I spelled out the words on my communication board, FILET MIGNON.

Mom repeated it, and Charlotte laughed easily, now relieved!

Twenty-two

Me, Get Dressed?

As the days and weeks passed, I was really ready to get out of the hospital. However, I was forgetting something. I hadn't begun to complete the impossible task of getting dressed!

Everything I had once taken for granted now became very precious to me. Needing help with the simplest of tasks, I was determined not to let it bother me. Many failures did occur, but only from these defeats did successes ever come.

One morning Carol from O.T. came to start my dressing lessons.

"It's the job of the occupational therapist," she explained, "to teach you activities of daily living such as getting dressed."

The nurses got me out of bed, and Carol immediately began her duty of re-training me to dress myself.

"First," she said, "You need to get out of the hospital gown. Try to get it off your shoulders."

I tried, but I couldn't get my right arm high enough. Carol helped me get my left arm out of the gown. Then it was time for the right arm. She coached me. "In order to get your right arm out, hold the gown between your legs."

The problem was, I couldn't hold my knees together tight enough, and the gown kept slipping out from my knees. Because of this, I couldn't get my arm out of the armhole. Carol let me try a few times on my own, and then she helped me.

"Next, we'll do your underwear. I'll refer to your left leg as your bad leg. Try to remember that your bad side goes first for just about everything. Pick your bad leg up and cross it over your good leg."

With Carol helping and after many tries, I was halfway there. But I just couldn't reach far enough. *I need extensions on my arms.*

When I couldn't get my foot near my hand, she said, "Tomorrow I'll bring you a 'reacher'."

Whatever that is.

Then we worked on putting on the rest of my clothes, down to my pants. The only thing left was my socks. Whoever thought getting dressed would be such an impossible task.

Oh, brother! This is so hard!

At one point, I looked down at myself, and I was totally distracted by a rubber tube coming out of my stomach.

Yuk! What is this? It's coming out of me!

Tracing the tube with my eyes, I realized it led upward to a bottle on an IV hanger.

It doesn't hurt. I don't even feel anything! I've noticed the nurses fiddling with bottles up there, but I didn't know they were attached to me! What's this for? I can ask Ruth.

"Are you getting tired?" Carol finally asked.

I shook my head no.

She said, "Then let's put on your socks. We'll do the bad leg first."

She helped me cross my legs and demonstrated as she spoke, "Get all five of your fingers in the leg of the sock, and then open your fingers as wide as you can."

Demonstrating on my foot, she said, "With your fingers spread out, get the sock around all five of your toes. Don't forget you have to get it around your baby toe too."

Beginning to try this, I almost fell out of the wheelchair.

With that, Carol said, "Okay, I'll get you dressed the rest of the way."

Good, I am getting tired.

Before I gave up, though, I was determined to put on my own deodorant. But after a while, I gave up. Holding the container with my knees, I couldn't even take the top off.

I'll be able to do this one day soon.

The next morning Carol came in with this odd-looking pole and asked, "Are you ready to get started?"

I nodded my head yes.

"I brought a reacher," she said. She held it before me and pulled the trigger. This caused the jaws to open.

She explained, "See, the reacher has a mouth-like device on the end of the pole that can grab things."

She picked up my shirt to demonstrate further. "Here, you try."

Having to really concentrate on pulling the trigger, I was able to move the mouth of the reacher, but my shirt was too heavy for me to pick up.

Carol said, "Well, maybe at first you can just use it to help you get dressed. Why don't you give it back to me, and we'll use it in a few minutes."

She brought a pair of pants closer to the wheelchair so I could hold them.

"You can wear your own pants now," she said. 'Your husband brought you some from home."

At least I won't look like a jailbird anymore!

"Let's see if you can put your pants on now."

Do I have to cross my legs again?

She answered as if reading my mind, "Cross your legs, grab your pants with your hand near the left hole, and then try to put your foot in the pants."

Carol had to help me cross my legs, and I was able to get my foot in.

Carol exclaimed, "Very good! You did it!"

I leaned back in the chair and let out a big sigh.

Carol continued, "Now, use the reacher as if it were your hand to grab the pants. Make sure you pull them up a little at a time or else you won't be able to pull them up at all."

Soon I was trying to get my other leg in, but after a few attempts, Carol had to help me. Again, I used the reacher to pull up the pants. Finally, I got them halfway on. She helped me stand up, and she pulled my pants up and fastened them.

Flopping down in my seat, I felt as if I'd worked all day.

Well, I don't have a shirt or shoes on. I'm exhausted! I feel like going out in the hallway just like this.

Noticing my fatigue, Carol said, "We're almost done. I'll put your shirt and shoes on with a little help from you."

Good!

She put the shirt on me, and I noticed the tube again.

That's right. I have to ask Ruth about this tube in my stomach.

There were buttons down the front of the shirt, and she said, "I would like you to try one button while I do the others."

Is this ever hard! I can't even do one button. I remember when I first got here, and I was watching Muriel, one of my former roommates get dressed. Now I understand why she was whining that day I was watching her get dressed.

When Carol finished with five buttons, I still hadn't done one. She had to do it for me.

The shoes were next. Feeling like a baby, I couldn't even push my left foot into the shoe. She had to wiggle it back and forth quite a few times in order for me to get it on.

Soon I was ready for the day's activities. Carol said, "It's only 8:30. I looked on the schedule and you don't have speech until 9:00. Do you want to go back to bed?"

Nodding, I thought, *I'm exhausted. I feel like it's the end of the day.*

Carol put me back to bed and said, "You did a good job, Laura," as she patted me on the hand. "See you later."

And to think I had always thought getting dressed was easy!

Twenty-three

Probably Nothing Serious – But I Can't Eat or Talk!

I felt comfortable enough with Ruth to ask her about the tube. In fact, I felt at ease at Lutheran General Hospital with everyone; they were all my friends. But I was still ready to get out of the hospital!

I pointed out the letters on my communication board: QUESTION.

Ruth said, "Okay."

Then she noticed something new. "Hey, you aren't using the sling anymore!" She sat down and asked, "Do you want me to take the sling off your wheelchair?"

Shaking my head no, I pointed, QUESTION.

Acknowledging my persistence, she inquired, "What do you want to ask me?"

WHY DO I HAVE THIS TUBE?

"You don't know?" she asked, stunned.

I shook my head no.

"Do you remember having surgery at Northwest Community Hospital?"

Thinking while semi-nodding, I was unsure. *I think I do. That seems like such a long time ago.*

Noticing my indecisiveness, Ruth explained, "It's a feeding tube. You had a gastrostomy. The surgeon put a tube in your stomach so you can be fed. You aren't able to eat yet ...on your own.

So, that's it! A feeding tube is what the doctors put in. That's what happened when I thought the doctors were going to chop off my breasts! I've been so busy since then that I haven't thought about it! How silly of me not to realize I wasn't eating like the rest of the human race! I pointed to the letters: IV.

"No, you don't have an IV any longer. That liquid from the bottle on the IV pole now goes straight into your stomach. It's your food."

She waited awhile for me to grasp all of this.

"Any more questions?"

I shook my head no as I thought, *The doctors at Northwest Community Hospital do know what they're doing.*

"While I'm telling you the facts," she went on, "I might as well continue. You have a condition, which is secondary to the stroke, known as dysarthria."

I pointed, HOW DO YOU SPELL IT?

She answered, "D-Y-S-A-R-T-H-R-I-A." She went on, "Many stroke patients have aphasia, which is the inability to process language. Charlotte, your roommate, has aphasia. Dysarthria affects the muscles of speech."

I nodded yes, as I listened intently.

"The muscles involved in speech - your lips, tongue, soft palate and diaphragm, etc. -" Ruth continued, " are paralyzed."

Ruth took a deep breath and sighed. Then she added, "Your soft palate and the reflex that makes you gag are completely paralyzed. I've been trying to stimulate them with an ice cold blunt instrument. Because your soft palate is paralyzed, it doesn't move at all when you speak. All the pressure you build up for speech goes right out your nostrils."

Nodding for yes, I thought, *WOW! I didn't know when I talk my soft palate is supposed to move! Mine doesn't move? Come on, soft palate - MOVE! There must be something I can do.*

Ruth went on, "I've been using ice to help stimulate your soft palate. This metal probe that I use at the back of your throat is a laryngeal mirror. I let it get cold in a cup of ice and then I lightly stroke the back of your throat."

I pointed, CAN I USE ICE?

"Definitely. I'll make sure you have ice in your room after therapy. You know that when I hold your nose, you have more air pressure coming out of your mouth. Remember the other day, I brought in some matches, and you were able to blow out one while I held your nose?

I nodded.

"The air goes right out your nose, and that's why I held your nose." She finished, "Does all of this make sense?"

Nodding my head again, I thought, *I know I'm not dreaming all of this. But how can this be happening?*

Again she took in a deep breath and asked, "What about this sling? Do you need it?"

In a trance, I shook my head no.

"Can I take it off?"

Mechanically nodding my head yes, I was still dazed by what she had just told me.

Ruth got the sling off, and she brought me out of my stupor by asking sarcastically, "Are you ready for your favorite contraption?"

It's called an incentive spirometer to help me breathe, because my diaphragm was mainly paralyzed. It resembled a round tube about a foot high and six inches wide, inside of which was an accordion-pleated cylinder. From the top of this was a flexible hose about two feet long, ending with a mouth piece for me to use to breathe into. Gradation lines on the sides measured my progress.

Using it didn't hurt at all, but I felt humiliated by Ruth having to hold my lips over the mouth piece because they were not strong enough to make a good seal. She also had to hold my nose with her other hand because my fingers weren't strong enough to do it myself. With all this help, the progress was non-existent.

I hate this thing!

Today was no different from any of the others. We also practiced vowel sounds, lip closure, and tongue movements.

I do notice some improvement with other exercises, but not with the spirometer.

I was anxious to learn about the ice in order to get my soft palate functioning again. Quickly, I pointed, ICE.

While looking at her watch, Ruth said, "I guess we could go down to your room now."

She pushed me in the wheelchair back to my room and went to get a cup of ice and a spoon. When she returned, I listened eagerly to her instructions. "Get the spoon cold and touch it to the back of your throat. Can you do that?"

Clumsily, I put the spoon into the cup of ice. Leaving it there for a minute, I almost knocked the cup over when I took the spoon out.

"Whoops --- almost!" Ruth exclaimed. She demonstrated on herself using a hand mirror so that I would know exactly the right area to stimulate. She gave me instructions. "Do it only three times, a couple times a day, otherwise you might OVER-stimulate it. Are you able to get the spoon back that far?"

She watched me painstakingly get it to the back of my throat and said, "Good. I'll let the nurses know what the ice and the spoon are for."

Learning this from Ruth was a big leap forward. She said, "I'll push you into the bathroom by the mirror because I need my hand mirror back. See you later."

She left me alone to practice.

Soon Chong came to get me for group.

Twenty-Four

So This Is What Therapy Is Like

After group therapy, Chong pushed me back to my room and looked at my schedule saying, "Diane should be here to get you for physical therapy. Should I put you in the hallway?"

I nodded yes.

"See you later."

While waiting for Diane, I was greeted by one of Charlotte's nurses, Linda. She said, "Charlotte just went down to a different floor. She had another stroke."

Noticing my concerned look, she said, "We hope she'll be all right. Well, I have to go."

I hope Charlotte is okay. She's such a nice person.

Suddenly, Diane appeared asking, "You ready for P.T.?"

Giving my head one distinct nod, I pointed, LETS GO.

Diane questioned, "No sling?"

I shook my head no.

She exclaimed, "Great!"

She pushed me into the physical therapy room where I exercised for a while and then she held a clear plastic leg brace,

"Your left foot has what we call foot drop. This brace fits into your shoe and it will hold your foot up to make it easier when you walk."

I nodded my head yes.

She put the brace and my foot into the shoe. We went out into the hallway to the parallel bars. They are not bars set up high like in gymnastics. They are two bars about 3½ - 4 feet high, 10 feet long, and about 3 feet apart. The height can be adjusted. I waited while Diane gave instructions to another patient.

Carolyn walked by and said, "Hi, Laura."

I nodded my head yes.

As if remembering something, she stopped, backed up, and asked, "Are you going on the parallel bars in a few minutes?"

I nodded my head yes again.

She said, "I wonder if I could take you for a walk. I'll have to find Diane and ask her."

In the hallway right outside physical therapy, many stroke survivors were waiting for their therapist to take them for a walk. One therapist walked up to a patient sitting in a wheelchair and said, "You're not going to use the quad cane anymore." The therapist smiled at the patient with excitement in her eyes, "This is what you'll use," as she held up a straight cane.

Then I looked down the hall and saw a patient walking with no assistance from the therapist. The therapist was walking beside the patient and they were talking nonchalantly. *He's using a straight cane, too.* Looking around at all the activity, I realized that all the patients were old. *Isn't there anyone near my age? The only one I've seen so far is John R., and he was in a car accident. I guess I'm not like these old people.*

Carolyn and Diane walked over and Diane said, "Carolyn is going to take you for a walk in the parallel bars. Okay?"

I nodded my head yes and then Diane went back to another patient.

Carolyn said, "We're going to wait for Dr. Lee. She just came back from vacation, and she wants to see what you can do now."

Soon Dr. Lee came in saying, "Hi, Laura. How are you?"

Nodding my head yes, I spelled, HOW WAS YOUR VACATION?

She replied, smiling and nodding, "Oh, fine, fine, fine. Let me see you walk."

Carolyn looked at me with wide eyes, as she asked, "Are you ready?"

I nodded yes.

Carolyn wheeled me to one end of the parallel bars, she set my communication board on the floor, and had me sit on the edge of the wheelchair seat. She said, "Okay, on the count of three. 1, 2, 3."

Up I went. She did most of the work, but I helped as much as I could. The main thought I had was that *this right leg has to hold me up.*

I grabbed the bar nearest me as tightly as I could while she moved my left leg forward. After she placed my foot carefully on the floor, rapidly I shuffled my right foot forward. Inch by inch, we made it one way. Carolyn asked, "Do you want to sit down?"

I shook my head.

"You want to make it a round trip?"

Up and down went my head.

We made it up and back, and I plopped down in the wheelchair in sheer exhaustion. Dr. Lee cheered, "All right, Laura. You did it!"

I didn't think I had performed any great feat but seeing the excitement and jubilation in their eyes was enough to get me to start laughing. The sound that came out of me was truly obnoxious, but they chuckled with pleasure at the progress I was making.

Dr. Lee and Carolyn left saying, "We'll let Diane know that you went for a walk."

Diane was very busy that day. She hustled back and forth,

from one patient to another. At one point, she came over saying, "I bet you're tired."

Nodding my head and rolling my eyes, I pointed, I AM BEAT.

She brought me to my room, to my bed, and put the brakes on the wheelchair as if she was going to put me into bed. *What are you doing, Diane?*

She took the communication board away and set it on the floor. I made a grunting sound while shaking my head.

She asked, "No? You don't want to go back to bed?"

Firmly, I shook my head no. Sometimes just sitting in the chair was enough to make me feel rested.

Diane said, "Okay."

She put me out in the hallway and said, "I don't know if I'll be able to see you this afternoon. We're so busy. I'll let you know. See you later," as she quickly walked away.

The slow parade of patients began filing down the hall. *What is that smell? It smells like food. I haven't eaten in a long time. I'm not hungry, but it sure smells good. It's lunchtime. I guess everyone is going to the dining room.*

Carolyn gave me a washcloth soaked in water and wrung it out for me to suck on. Ruth walked by, pointing at it and said, "That is a really good idea. You can develop your sucking reflex. That way maybe you'll be able to eat sooner."

Feeling sorry for me, Carolyn sometimes would barely wring out the washcloth. When she would hand me a wet cloth, barely wrung out I would snatch it from her as if I were on a desert island with no water. Sucking away at my terry cloth lunch as best I could, I felt partially satisfied. *This isn't food, but it'll do.*

Linda walked over and said "What's that?"

I held it out for her to see.

She said, "No. Tell me," pointing a finger down at my communication board.

I pointed, AWASHCLOTH.

She said, "Maybe you could do something between words, so

they don't run together." She thought for a few seconds, then asked, "Can you pound your fist down like this?" as she demonstrated on my communication board. "Try it."

This time, I pointed, A # WASHCLOTH.

"That's good," she said, "why don't you do that from now on?"

In total agreement, I pointed, I # SURE # WILL.

Carolyn called out, "Linda, can you help me?"

Linda replied, "I have to go," quickly jogging down the hallway.

The exhaustion I felt earlier settled upon me again like waves splashing upon the seashore, coming and going with each distraction.

I can't stay up any longer. I have to go to bed and rest.

The next time Carolyn walked by I signaled to her. She came over asking, "What's up?"

Totally drained, I pointed, BED.

She asked, "You want to go back to bed?"

I nodded my head a definite yes.

She put me back and I felt instant relief from my tired, aching muscles. She said, "Let me check the schedule and see when your next therapy session is," rushing out of the room. When she came back, she said, "You have speech therapy at 1:00. It's 12:30 now so you have a half hour to rest," walking out of the room.

Relishing the idea of having a full half hour to rest, I was suddenly sparked with a revelation. I can change the channels on the TV because I have a regular remote control. Grabbing the new nurses' call light/TV remote control, I turned the TV on and changed the channel to my favorite soap opera. A commercial was on so I played around with the buttons. Yesterday the nurses had me try to push the buttons on the regular remote control and I could do it. They replaced the squeezable call light with one of the "normal" remotes. *I haven't seen this soap opera in a long time. The nurses at Northwest Community Hospital would put it on, but I could only listen to it. Now I can see it. The double vision is gone.*

The soap opera was almost over when Carolyn came in again saying, "It's almost time for therapy. Up and at 'em!"

A half hour was just enough time for me to refill my energy stores. She got me out of bed and I was off to speech therapy. After that, I had occupational therapy.

The O.T. room hummed with activity. Here the patients were not exercising their legs and walking around; they were pulled up to tables in their wheelchairs working on arm, hand, and finger movements. Carol pushed me to an open area and asked, "Do you remember these?" as she pointed to those all-too-familiar cardboard cones.

I nodded my head. *Of course I do. I still wear one on my left hand at night. They're a little bit different.*

She said, "What I want you to do is to try to extend your right arm to where I have put the cones."

They were within my reach, but I really had to stretch.

During the middle of the exercise, Diane walked in and said, "I won't be able to see you this afternoon because we're so busy. Okay?"

Nodding my head yes, I dropped a cone. *I guess I can't do two things at the same time.*

Diane said in a hurry, "See you tomorrow."

Managing a slow, deliberate wave, I nodded my head to let her know I understood. *Okay, Diane.*

I finished up that exercise and Carol had me do many others with my right hand. On my left hand, my fingers tingled but they wouldn't budge. Soon our session was over and she took me back to my room asking, "Do you want to stay out in the hall?"

Nodding my head yes, *I want to stay in my chair and rest, and in a little while, I'll practice going around the nurses' station.*

After putting me against the wall so I could see the people walking by, she said, "Remember, I won't be here early tomorrow to help you get dressed because your husband and your mom will be here for training. I'll see you later in the day."

Completing my early evening ritual of going around the nurses' station, I motioned Carolyn to come. I felt as if I had just run the 100 yard dash three times in a row. Exhausted, I pointed, BED.

She asked, "You want to go to bed?"

I nodded.

Adding sarcastically with a smile, she said, "All we ever do all day is put you into bed and take you out of bed."

Laughing on the inside, I was too weak to laugh on the outside. I just nodded my head.

Twenty-Five

Where Is Mom?

After resting for an hour, I confidently pressed the nurses' call button and Mary Joy came in. Motioning like a hitchhiker wanting a ride, *I need to get out of this bed NOW. It's already 5:00pm, and Mom should already be here.*

Mary Joy got me out of bed and asked, "Do you want to go out in the hall?"

I shook my head no. *It's almost supper time. I can smell the food when I'm in the hall. It's not that I'm hungry, but the food smells so good.* To keep myself occupied, I watched some TV and did some occupational therapy exercises Carol had given me.

It's 5:30 and still no sign of Mom. *I'm sure she said she'd be here tonight. Usually she comes right after work. I think she gets home about 4:00. She doesn't live far from the hospital.* I watched more TV while practicing speech exercises.

It's 6:00! Where IS she? This is how she must have felt when I went out on a date! Doing more of my exercises, I was running out of things to do. Not really interested in the TV, I began looking around my room for something to do. "The Readers' Digest" that Chong had left me caught my eye. Paging through it, I wasn't interested in any of the articles. Although, this time I could see them.

It's nearly 6:30! Where is Mom? Starting to feel sorry for myself, I began thinking of everything I couldn't do.

Soon Mary Joy walked in, surprised, saying, "Are you still here by yourself? No one has come to visit you yet?"

My tender emotions couldn't handle anymore, and I burst out crying.

She rushed over to comfort me saying, "Oh, I'm sorry. Is someone coming to visit you?"

Nodding, I thought, *Yes, and she should have been here hours ago!*

She asked, "Who is coming? Your mom?"

I nodded yes, still crying loudly.

She said, "I'm sure if she said she'd be here, she'll be here."

I wasn't able to think that possibly Mom could have been in a car accident. All I considered was that she was supposed to be here to visit ME.

Mary Joy tried to cheer me up, but it was an impossible task. Soon Mom came walking in with my Aunt Betty and Uncle Ken trailing behind. With a concerned look, Mom said, "We could hear you crying all the way from inside the elevator. Are you upset that we weren't here earlier?"

I tried not to cry anymore, and I nodded my head yes.

She came over and gave me a hug saying, "Oh, Hon. I'm so sorry. We went out for dinner. I should have called the nurses' station."

Mary Joy said, "She thought you weren't coming."

Mom said, "I would have let someone know if I couldn't make it."

Aunt Betty and Uncle Ken had concerned looks on their faces, too, as they came over to greet me giving me with a hug and a kiss. They said, "Laura, we're sorry."

All is forgiven! At least, you're here now!

Mary Joy left saying, "I'm glad you're here."

Uncle Ken changed the subject to try to stop my crying, he asked, "How are they treating you around here?"

Wiping the tears away, I nodded, which meant fine.

Mary Joy came back in saying, "I forgot my pen," as she grabbed it off my bedside table.

"Laura," Uncle Ken quickly replied, "I bet this is the drill sergeant," as he motioned to Mary Joy. "She probably keeps everyone in line," his nose wrinkled, his shoulders heaved with hearty laughter.

"You'd better believe it," giggled Mary Joy!

"Oh," said Uncle Ken, "One of those," he continued laughing.

Mary Joy nodded and smiled.

He asked, "Do you like to stay out late?"

Aunt Betty immediately interjected, "Ken, stop it."

Mary Joy replied, "I'd rather not answer that question on the grounds that it might incriminate me," Mary Joy said, enjoying the nonsense that was going on between them.

He raised his hand as if to set a halt to all that was going on, he asked with a smile, "Pleading the fifth, huh?"

Nodding yes, Mary Joy walked out of the room.

After much clowning around, which was usually the case when Uncle Ken was around, they conversed seriously about my stroke. Uncle Ken said, "It could have happened to anyone."

It could have? But why me?

Soon Mike came in. Uncle Ken, Aunt Betty, and Mom stayed about an hour longer, and then they left. Mike was his jovial self, cheering me up seemed to be his main concern.

Twenty-six

Strip Poker

After Aunt Betty, Uncle Ken, and Mom left, Mike asked, "Do you want to go down to the lounge to play a game?"

Enthusiastically, I nodded.

Mike said, "Remind me my keys are on your dresser."

We went down to the lounge, which had the lingering smell of food because it posed as the dining room during mealtimes. *I wish I could eat.*

Mike was looking at all the games when he came across this block of wood with slits in it. He asked a patient nearby, "Do you know what this is?"

The patient said, "It's a card holder with slits in it for the cards. It's for stroke patients who only have use of one hand."

"I see," said Mike.

The man replied pointing, "And over there are some cards."

"Thank you," said Mike. "Look, we can play cards," he said to me with excitement in his dark brown eyes. "Do you want to play strip poker?"

I was preoccupied with the card holder so I just nodded.

Surprised, he asked, "You do?"

Looking at him with what I imagined was a dumb look, I thought, *I do what?*

He exclaimed, "You want to play strip poker!"

Laughing, I shook my head.

After a few games of cards, Mike and I went back to the room to watch TV. As he was leaving, I spelled, DONT # FORGET # YOU # ARE # SUPPOSED # TO # COME # TOMORROW.

He quickly replied, "Oh, that's right. I didn't forget, it just slipped my mind. I'm supposed to watch you during therapy, so I can learn how to transfer you in the wheelchair. Mom is coming, too."

Excitedly, I nodded yes.

He said, looking at the clock, "Well, I better go. It's almost 8:00."

Giving me a kiss, he walked toward the door. I carefully and slowly motioned for him to come here and then I pointed, YOUR # KEYS.

His eyes lit again as it dawned on him, "Oh, that's right." Picking them up off the dresser, he said, "I wouldn't get very far without these." Looking at me quizzically, he said, "You have the memory of an elephant."

Laughing, I just shrugged my shoulders. I consciously waved to him, thinking and watching all four fingers together down – up, down – up, and down – up – down.

He called out, "Hey, that's good. See you tomorrow."

As soon as he left, I pressed the call button for the nurses. Mary Joy came in asking, "How was your visit?"

I nodded fine.

"You have a very nice family," she replied. Sitting on my bed, she said, "You had a hard day. Do you want to go to bed?"

Forcefully, I nodded yes again.

She said, "Okay," and put me to bed.

The week-ends were sometimes very nice because I got visits from my out of town relatives. My sister, Christie and her husband,

Frank and their two girls, Gina (age 8) and Margot (age 5) came from near Indianapolis, Indiana. It was nice to see them.

We went into the lounge and talked. I should say that I just pointed.

The next morning, I was awakened by a young man in a white coat who was an employee. He said, "Laura Barnett, I'm here to get a blood sample."

I used to do that. The patients I would draw blood from knew me as the early morning vampire. Trying to start a conversation with him, I opened my mouth and nothing would come out. It was like when I had a nightmare, and I wanted to scream, but not one sound would pass my lips. That's right. I can't talk. I'll be able to someday, though. I pretended I was sleeping until the man was gone.

Soon Marilyn came in to get me up. After dressing me, she helped me in the bathroom and then put me out in the hallway. *Mike and Mom should be here pretty soon. I can't wait for them to get here!*

That day, Mike and Mom came, and Mike pushed me to all of my therapy sessions. Directing him with my one useful hand, I felt like a queen in a chauffeur-driven limousine.

Mike and Mom learned a lot that day: how to transfer me on and off the toilet, how to transfer me into and out of the wheelchair, how to feed me and care for my tube, and how to help me with the many exercises. Now I was ready to go home on a day pass.

TWENTY-SEVEN

Call Me Cinderella

The week went slowly as I anticipated my first day pass. It was like a count-down to lift off! When the day finally came, I woke up early that Saturday morning. I was so excited! I could feel my pulse in both ears. It seemed to take the nurses forever to get me out of bed. Finally, I was up and ready to go. It was only 8:00 am and Mike wasn't coming until 9:45. Having almost two hours to waste, I practiced going around the nurses' station; then I waited at the elevator. It kept stopping at my floor and strangers spilled out. *Hurry up, Mike. I can't wait to go home!*

He finally came about 9:30, and Marilyn gave him a refresher course on how to feed me and care for the feeding tube. We were finally ready to go. Mike loaded me in my wheelchair with all my paraphernalia, burying my face so I could hardly see. We both tried to balance a Connect Four game someone had given me, but it toppled to the floor. Marilyn picked it up and carefully placed it on the haphazard pile. Mike looked at the bed and noticed how much more we had to take. He made a quick decision. "Let me take this stuff downstairs to the pick-up truck first. Marilyn, can you meet me down there with Laura?"

She said, "Sure."

Mike went ahead of us as I waved my good-byes to the nursing staff. Outside, Marilyn and I waited for Mike to pull up in the red pick-up. The air smelled so fresh and clean. *It's so warm out. That's right. Being cooped up in this hospital, I forgot that it's July. I love the summer season, and it's slipping away.*

Mike pulled up, and he loaded my gear into the back of the truck. He picked me up and placed me in the passenger seat as if he had been doing this for 20 years. Marilyn laughed, "Mike, it's good she's skinny, or you'd be in trouble."

Looking at me, Mike said, "You better not EVER gain any weight."

He put the empty wheelchair in the back and hopped in the driver's seat. We said goodbye, and off we went. I felt like Cinderella being carried off by her prince.

The ride home took about an hour, and we listened to music on the radio while Mike sang along. He snapped his fingers in time to the music saying, "You try."

I can do that! It's easy! When I tried, I couldn't make a sound. In fact, my fingers didn't even go together for the snap. I had to think about touching my middle finger with my thumb, pushing them together as hard as I could and at the same time sliding them apart so I could make that "clicking" sound. I kept looking at Mike's hand to see how he did it. *I used to do this without even thinking. Is there anything I can do that doesn't take work?* Looking down at my fingers and concentrating, I felt something wet on my hand. *What's this? Oh, I'm drooling again.* Wiping it as best I could with the back of my hand, I went back to finger snapping. Practicing that for quite a while, I was starting to get frustrated.

Mike said, "Can you tap your right foot?"

Trying with my right foot, I could feel my toes move, but I couldn't see my foot move. Now, I had something else to practice. Mike had me try to snap my fingers and tap my foot in time to the music. Even with practice, I was still unsuccessful.

When we arrived home, we pulled into the driveway, and I stared in shock at the gaslight post.

This is where it all began! I can't believe it!

Mike took the wheelchair out of the back, pulled it up to the passenger seat and hauled me out of the truck. Hearing the dogs' bark, I was just as excited to see them as they were to see me. Mike opened the door and firmly said, "Stay." The dogs paused, but their tails wagged furiously. Not being able to contain themselves any longer, they both jumped in my lap on the wheelchair and began licking my face. Mike closed the door behind us and scolded them while shooing them off my lap, "Okay, guys. Let us in the house. Then you can see her."

What a happy moment! Once we were inside, the dogs were free to greet me. Scraps' high-pitched squeal said he knew it was me, but Megan, who was still a puppy was wagging her tail furiously. She thought I was just another visitor. When they realized that I was going to stay, they simmered down and went about their business.

Looking around the house, I thought, *the house looks the same, yet different somehow.*

Mike said, "A neighbor has been coming over and doing the housework, and whatever else I don't get around to."

It looks pretty good.

Looking out into the back yard, I suddenly remembered the flower garden. In May, I was going to plant some petunias in the back right after our neighbor, Tom and I planted the ones in front. Needless to say, I never got around to it.

From where I was sitting, I couldn't see the flower garden. I imagined weeds growing in the circular space set apart from the grass by rocks. Mike asked, "What are you looking at?"

I pointed on the board, THE # FLOWER # GARDEN.

He said, "I'll move you closer to the window so you can see it." He pushed a chair out of the way. I craned my head to look. No weeds! Just beautiful purple and pink petunias!

Mike said, "Tom, next-door, planted them."

I pointed, THAT # WAS # NICE.

Mike nodded. "Look in the back at your vegetable garden. Remember? You planted that."

That's right. It seems like such a long time ago. Wow! Are those plants tall!

Laughing, Mike asked, "Remember when you planted cucumbers by the neighbor's fence behind us? He came out and told you not to put them so close to his fence. You came in crying saying, 'That man doesn't want me to plant cucumbers by his fence.'"

Laughing along with him, I thought, *how could I have been so upset about cucumbers?*

"Last month we had so many strawberries my mom had to freeze some."

I planted a big garden.

We went into the living room to watch TV. After one program Mike asked, "Do you want to lie down and rest?"

I nodded yes. Mike had to make some minor changes in the arrangement of our living room furniture so he could get my wheelchair next to the couch. He transferred me to the couch. *This feels so good!*

After about an hour, he transferred me back to the wheelchair. Soon there was a knock on the door. It was a delivery man with two bouquets of flowers.

"They're for you, Laura, from my boss and my co-workers."

I spelled out, HOW # NICE.

We had an uneventful day, but a peaceful one at that. At 6:30, reluctantly, Mike said, "It's time to go."

I started to cry. *I don't want to go. I wish I could stay.*

"Next week is your birthday. Dr. Lee already told me you could come home for that."

She did? I feel better at the thought of coming home again next week.

The drive back to the hospital seemed to go fast, too fast.

When we arrived, it seemed like I was never away. We had to be back by 8 pm or my insurance wouldn't cover the day.

The day was magic, and I continued to feel like Cinderella. Now my chariot was turning back into a pumpkin, and my gown was becoming my hospital clothes.

Twenty-Eight

And now Happy Birthday!

Two days before my birthday, Carol, my occupational therapist, said, "It'll be good practice for you to make your own cake. Baking with one hand can present quite a challenge. I want you to make your own birthday cake."

Nodding my head yes, *BUT...I can't even eat it!*

"First, we need to turn on the oven," as she handed me a box of chocolate cake mix. She pointed to the part of the instructions and read, 'Preheat the oven to 350 degrees.'

Nodding my head yes, I watched her, as she turned the oven on.

She said, "Let's both wash our hands." The sink was lower for wheelchairs, and she handed me a towel to dry my hand. "All you'll have to add is eggs, butter, and water." She handed me the cake mix, as she said, "Put the package between your legs and open it."

I tried to do as she instructed, but my legs weren't strong enough. The box kept slipping between my legs.

"Here let me help you," she took the package, opened it, and said, "Now take the package of cake mix out of the cardboard box."

Fumbling with it, I almost dropped it.

"You can use scissors to open the package of cake mix, but I'll open it for you. Put the cake mix into this big yellow bowl," as she handed me the mix.

I took it carefully, and she also held onto it. We both held onto it while we dumped the mix into the yellow bowl.

"Good job! Now crack one of these eggs on the side of this small bowl."

I tried tapping the egg on the side of the dish, but I didn't seem to have enough strength to crack it.

As she held onto the bowl, she said, "Now try tapping a little harder."

The shell cracked, and everything went into that little bowl. The white and yolk went in plus all of the shell that was now in tiny pieces.

Carol said, "That's okay! That's why we crack them in a separate bowl."

We spent the next few minutes fishing the egg shells out of the egg white and yolk mixture.

"Are you getting tired?"

I shook my head no.

"Well, I'll crack the other egg and put both of them in with the mix with the butter and water. I want you to use the mixer."

After she added all of the ingredients, she handed me a mixer. She showed me how to turn it on, and suggested I use the lowest speed setting.

While mixing the batter, I had to stop at least a dozen times to rest my arm. *Is this ever hard work!*

Carol could tell I was exhausted. She said, "I'll finish it. I'll take you back to your room. You did a great job, Laura."

And so I baked a cake. We had a party in the lounge the day before my birthday and six staff members showed up. Carol put some candles on the cake, lit them, and said, "Okay, blow them out."

I held my nose and blew out one solitary candle.

I feel victorious!

Everyone cheered and clapped. As they ate the luscious cake with gooey frosting, I sucked on a wet washcloth, and soon the party was over. Making sure that Charlotte got a piece of cake, I was glad she was my roommate again. She still had aphasia, but her second stroke paralyzed her right arm and leg. She was in a wheelchair now.

That evening when Mike came for a quick visit, he teased me about our imaginary marriage contract that required me not to get fat. He said, "Yeah, I almost broke my back last weekend lifting you into the pick-up." He motioned with his hand over his back as he walked all hunched over. "Thank goodness you can't eat, Laura, or you probably would have swallowed up your whole birthday cake."

After he went home, the nurses put me to bed. *Tomorrow is August 2. Who would have ever thought that I'd be in the hospital on my 24th birthday?*

I woke up early the next morning, eager for my Prince Charming to arrive in his chariot and whisk me away to our palace. A nurse helped me out of bed, and she got me dressed and all cleaned up. Once again, I waited for Mike at the elevators. The doors slid open, and there he was. We were off.

When we got home, I found the house decorated with crepe paper and balloons. Soon the guests began to arrive. Besides our families, both his and mine, he had invited many mutual friends. Among them was one who had learned she was pregnant before I had the stroke. I was surprised when I saw her because she looked as if she was ready to deliver any minute. Also, Nancy, my best girlfriend and Mark, her fiance were there. Seeing them was a reminder about their wedding. *That's right! They're getting married in April. I'm going to be in their wedding. I'll be well by then!*

They brought me a cake with 24 candles on it, already lit. This time I held my nose, huffed and puffed, but I couldn't blow out even one candle. Trying again, I still had no luck. Mom said, "That's okay. Here, open your presents."

After I opened the presents, everyone had cake, except me. It didn't matter, though, because I had my trusty washcloth. Since it was a special day, Mike dunked my washcloth into my favorite cocktail, a Seagram's Seven and 7-Up. *Does this ever taste good!*

Soon some of the guests began to leave, and I took a nap in the bedroom. When I woke up, we played cards. The only problem - I had left my card holder at the hospital. Mike had an alternate plan. He took an empty, small cardboard box, put the top inside the bottom, and that left a crack so the cards could be put into it. That was my ready-made card holder.

We decided to play UNO which requires the person with one card left to yell, "UNO!" Not being able to speak, I would yell, "UNO" by ringing a bell.

Before I knew it, it was time to return to the hospital. When we got back to the 6th floor, Mike talked to one of the nurses about my difficulty blowing out the candles today, and yesterday I was able to blow out one.

She said, "Oh, yes. All stroke survivors go through that. It can be one step forward and two steps back."

My special day was just about over.

This was so much fun! I wish this day would never end!

Yes, I was only 24, but it seemed I had already lived so many years. I thought back to my two birthday parties - today and yesterday - and to all the fun and Mike's loving care of me. I was happier than I had been in a long time.

Twenty-nine

Can I Eat or Can't I?

On August 19th, I was going to have a swallowing test. In medical lingo, it's called a video flouroscopy.

Ruth had told me about it the day before. "It's an X-ray to determine whether you can eat or not. A small amount of barium is swallowed in liquid-form; an X-ray is taken while it hopefully travels to the esophagus and not the windpipe."

Please, let me eat!

The radiology technician came with a wheelchair, transferred me to his wheelchair, and he took me to the radiology department. Another technician gave me a liquid to drink which she told me had barium in it. It really had no taste and before I knew it, the test was over. The technician said, "Your speech therapist will review the results with your doctor and then one of them will let you know the outcome."

She took me back to my room, not giving me any indication of the results of the test. I was on pins and needles. *I have an hour before speech therapy. Ruth told me she would tell me the results. Can I eat - or can't I? I want to know.*

Finally, it was time for speech therapy. Ruth had a cafeteria tray in her office, so I knew the verdict. *Yes, I can eat!*

She said, "I want to watch you while you eat and drink, keeping an eye on your swallowing. Right now, we'll feed you by the tube to make sure you get enough nutrition. You have a restriction on your diet: only pureed food (mashed up in a blender) or baby food."

I don't care! Let me eat! I'm not hungry, but I feel as if I could devour a dinosaur!

Ruth gave me a sip of apple juice, and it slid down with no problem. Then I took a bigger sip and starting choking and coughing. Quickly, she took it away with a concerned look and said, "I think what happens with liquids is they rush down the back of your throat. You don't have time to swallow them, and you choke. You're going to have to take it slower than slow."

Next she gave me some mashed potatoes.

Mm, they taste so good! I wish I could eat more, but I'm stuffed.

Ruth said, "I'll order a tray tomorrow for lunch."

Hooray! Finally, I can have a tray!

I left and went about my daily routine. When the patients went down to the dining room, I called a nurse over and I pointed to my communication board:

I # WANT # 7-Up.

She smiled and said, "Gladly."

Soon I ate in the hallway by the dining room, so the nurses could keep an eye on me. My coughing and choking persisted, mostly with liquids, but that didn't stop me. By the end of August, I was eating three mini-meals a day.

Thirty

Spaghetti Splash

On one of my day passes, Mike and our Moms were at our house and we were about to have lunch. The kitchen was a small area with an aisle running through the middle of it with an eating area attached. I was watching Mike and the Moms fix our lunch. My mom was going to the refrigerator dodging Mike as he walked through carrying the blender. Mike's mom was making spaghetti, and she tested the noodles to see if they were ready.

Mike began mashing up a portion of the noodles with the red sauce in the blender for me. He was bending over it looking inside at the contents. Suddenly, he had spaghetti all over the ceiling. He slowly turned to look at me, and it was all over his face! Immediately, I burst out laughing, which caused the two Moms to look, and when they saw Mike's spaghetti splashed over the kitchen counter, walls and ceiling, they joined in the laughter.

Mike's sister Phyllis and her husband Sam walked in right at that moment. Their faces dropped in shock. Sam blurted out, "What happened?"

Mike sheepishly said, "Well, the spaghetti was stuck to the

side of the blender in clumps, and I just stuck a fork in to mix it up."

Phyllis asked, disbelieving, "With it still running?"

Mike replied, "Yes, and the fork got caught in the blades."

Everyone in the room exclaimed, "Ohhhh."

Thirty-one

Off to the Races!

During the following few weeks, I began eating foods like ground steak and potatoes but no raw foods. I also began printing words on paper, going home on day passes both days of the weekend, getting dressed by myself, except for my shoes and brace, and taking a shower with little assistance from a nurse.

I felt good about myself, but I knew I was far from where I wanted to be. After all, I couldn't speak, I had the feeding tube dangling from my side (only for medication), and worst of all, I was still in the wheelchair. *I'm not going home in this thing.*

Nancy reiterated my feelings when one evening she said, "You can't come down the aisle in a wheelchair at my wedding."

On my paper, I printed, I know.

From that moment on, I had a renewed motivation to get out of that chair. Whenever Mike visited me, I printed to him to help me practice walking. Whenever a nurse didn't seem busy, I printed, Can you take me for a walk?

One evening Mike was helping me walk down the hall, holding my left arm while I used a quad cane with my right. I tried to remember everything Diane had told me: *Look straight ahead, keep the cane out of the way of my right foot, try not to take steps that are too big, and try not to walk pigeon-toed.*

We met our objective and were heading back to my room. With all my concentration, I began to drool. Mike said jokingly, "Let's see if that drool will hit the floor."

Feeling giddy already, I laughed hysterically.

He continued joking, "Look ... look ... there it goes ..."

My fog horn laugh was still obnoxious. What made matters worse, as I turned the corner to enter my room, there was my brother Mike sitting on my bed waiting for us. He was laughing at our silliness, which made me laugh harder. The more I laughed, the more I drooled. My stomach muscles just couldn't take the laughing. Leaning and holding onto the bathroom door, I was afraid to let go or else I would fall. My brother asked, "Do you want me to move the wheelchair closer?"

Mike waved him off saying, "No, no, no. She can make it."

I can? Trying very hard to compose myself, I made it back to the wheelchair, and plopped down with a sigh of relief. *Whew! I made it!*

We all laughed, and I grabbed a Kleenex to wipe my mouth. After a nice visit, both Mikes left.

As soon as they were gone, I took my card holder off my bedside table and went out to look for Charlotte to see if she or anyone else wanted to get a card game together. A young girl, Sandy who had MS, came up to me in her wheelchair and asked, "Do you want to play cards?"

I nodded yes.

She asked, "Who else wants to play?"

I shrugged my shoulders.

Looking around, she said, "I'll go see. We can play in my room. Go ahead down there, and I'll see if anyone else wants to play."

Sandy had a private room at the end of the hall because she was primarily independent. I made my way there; Sandy and Charlotte soon joined me. Sandy said, "Everyone else has gone to bed."

Charlotte stuttered while smiling, "W … we … uh … uh … we … uh … uh … are … uh … i … it."

Sandy said, "Yep," taking a deck of cards off her table.

Linda, the nurse, walked in and asked, "What's this? The three musketeers are playing cards?"

We played cards for a couple of hours. After the final game, Charlotte and I headed back to our rooms, rolling along in our wheelchairs, side by side.

Suddenly, Charlotte deliberately pulled out in front, grinning at me when she passed. Making my right arm and leg work like they never worked before, I passed her and took the lead. She just laughed and said, "I … I'll … uh … ge … get … uh … uh … you."

With that, she turned on the wheelchair steam. We were traveling side by side, determination etched in our faces. I couldn't hold the lead. My steam fizzled. After she took the lead once again, I had to stop, rest, and I let out a big sigh. Then she stopped and let out an even bigger sigh. We just laughed, pausing in the hallway to regroup our energies.

Nurse Linda met us in the hallway. She glanced at me and then at Charlotte, and then she laughed, "Did you two have a race?"

Charlotte and I nodded as we both gasped for air.

Linda asked, "Who won?"

I pointed at Charlotte.

"Very good," Linda said. "I suppose you two want to go to bed now?"

We both nodded.

"Well, the winner should go first."

Looking at me, she chirped, "Laura, next time you'll have to beat her."

I nodded.

After putting us both to bed, Linda turned on the television. *The Tonight Show* with Johnny Carson in our room, and before I knew it, Marilyn was nudging me saying, "It's morning, wake up. Laura, wake up. Dr. Lee is going to talk to you. She has good news!"

Dr. Lee came in smiling, "We had a staffing for you yesterday and it was decided that you can go home for good this Saturday, September 27!"

Yippee! Alright! All of this time in the hospital, I can finally go home. I'm so tired of this place! Let's see, three whole months here, and one month at Northwest Community Hospital for a total of four months. Finally, I can get out of this hospital!

She asked, still smiling, "Isn't that great?"

Laughing, I nodded.

"You should WALK into Dr Round's office and surprise the heck out of him."

Yes, that would shock Dr. Round. He hasn't see n me since I was at Northwest Community Hospital.

Marilyn asked, "Isn't that great? Aren't you excited?"

I nodded my head. *I know that I haven't yet accomplished all that I wanted to. Oh, well. I'll just have to exercise at home to get better.*

Dr. Lee said, "I'll arrange with Mike to have a nurse at home with you while he's at work."

A nurse? I'm sure I'll need her for a little while. After that, I'll be alright.

The next day during speech therapy, Ruth explained, "Since your soft palate is still paralyzed, there's a new device available; it's called a palatal lift. It's a retainer that lifts up the soft palate, with a big bulb in back that does the lifting. I'd like to see if you're a candidate for one."

That's nice, but I'm sure my soft palate will come back soon.

She asked, "Any questions?"

I printed to her, Can other people see it?

"No, not really," she said, "There are silver bands that are placed on four upper teeth, two on each side, which hold the lift in place. They are only visible when you smile. Okay?"

Nodding my head, I listened intently.

Ruth continued, "The dentists make it at the Dental School in downtown Chicago. It's called the Cleft Lip and Palate Institute. I'll let your family know the details."

I nodded my head up and down.

"Let's get to work!" She continued, "A normal soft palate moves up for the p, s, t, and many other sounds, but it doesn't move for the m, n, and ng sounds. Since your soft palate is paralyzed, the tones you make all sound like m, n, or ng. So b sounds like m, t sounds like n, and so on. Understand?"

I nodded.

She said, "Let's work on strengthening your tongue, lips, and diaphragm."

Ruth stimulated my soft palate with ice, and all I kept thinking was, *Come on soft palate. MOVE!*

When that session was over, I went to physical therapy. As I greeted Diane, she exclaimed, "Congratulations! You are graduating from a quad cane to a straight cane!"

Alright!

We tried out the new cane. I still needed her to hold onto my left arm for balance, but I felt there was some difference in the placement of the straight cane as opposed to the quad cane. It took a little getting used to, but soon I felt comfortable.

I still had a week before I went home. It seemed to go by so slowly! The days crept by. *I can't wait to get out of this place. I wish Saturday would hurry up!*

Thirty-Two

There's No Place Like Home

September 27, 1980 – I was finally getting discharged. Marilyn got me out of bed, although I had been lying awake for hours, too excited to go back to sleep. She had to help me to the bathroom, but I could do everything else by myself, except get my shoes and brace on.

Waiting at the elevators for Mike, I was so excited. Soon he came, and we were both thrilled for me to go home. We gathered up all my belongings, and I printed a note saying, LETS GET OUT OF HERE.

Mike agreed, and I said my goodbyes. Marilyn helped me downstairs while Mike loaded the truck with all my junk from a four-month hospital stay. Next Mike loaded me into the red pick-up truck We said goodbye to Marilyn, many of the other staff, and off we went. Looking back at her pushing the empty wheelchair, I had second thoughts, *Wait, Marilyn wait. I'm scared! It's really happening. I'm going to miss the tender loving care of the nurses.*

With that, I started crying.

Mike asked, "What's the matter?"

Shaking my head, I meant nothing. *How am I going to manage at home by myself? I know I won't be on my own, but I don't know any of the new nurses. Will they be as caring as Marilyn and Carolyn? And how am I going to do without a wheelchair? Oh, I remember, I'll have one at home, just in case. Mom said a friend is giving me one. I'll use it only if I have to. I guess maybe, I'll be fine.*

We drove along for a while. "Are you okay now?" Mike asked.

Drying my eyes, I nodded my head.

Soon I was self-doubting again. *Will I really be okay? I feel so safe at the hospital.*

Beginning to cry again, I sobbed hysterically. Mike asked, "What's wrong?"

Motioning to him, I wanted a pen and paper. He pulled over to the side of the road and got them out of the glove compartment.

I printed, I WILL MISS MANY OF THE NURSES.

He said, "I know you will Hon but won't it be great to be home?"

I nodded my head. *I'll be all right. I do want to go home! In fact, it's time for me to go home for good.*

Drying my eyes again, I pointed my finger straight ahead. Mike knew exactly what I meant because he put the truck in gear and off we went. "Away we go!" he shouted.

The first item on the agenda was to go over to Mom's house to get my wedding rings. Mom had taken them off of me when I was in a coma at Northwest Community Hospital because a nurse had said that anyone could have taken them.

As we pulled into Mom's driveway, she came out to the car with my rings. I tried to get them on, but the fingers on my left hand were clenched too tightly. I needed help. Mike pried my ring finger loose and put the rings on before my finger snapped closed like an alligator's jaw.

I'm married again!

Soon, we were on our way home. I was thrilled, but I was

apprehensive at the same time. I even tried singing with Mike. I sounded terrible because my voice had lost all pitch, inflection, and intelligibility. But now I could snap my fingers and tap my foot on my right side, all at the same time.

When we took a break from the joviality and singing, I began crying again, missing the nurses. Mike just let me cry. When we finally got home, he went inside to lock up the dogs so they wouldn't trip me. He came back out and helped me into the house, sat me down on a chair, and let the dogs loose. When he released them from their prison, they made a mad dash to see who had invaded their territory. Again, Scraps squealed with delight and Megan just sniffed me, both of them licking my face.

You know what, guys? I'm home to stay!

That evening, I was in the bedroom taking a nap, and when I woke up, I could hear Mike banging pots and pans in the kitchen. I rang a bell to let him know that I was awake, and he came in asking, "Do you want to get up now?"

I nodded.

He said, "Dinner's almost ready. You can sit at the kitchen table."

He helped me up, and we walked down the hall to the kitchen where I looked at the table and let out a soft, "Oh!"

"Welcome to Barnettelli's Restaurant!" Mike had it set for a candlelight dinner for two. Steak, baked potato, and buttered asparagus were on the menu. We sat down, and he cut everything into small pieces for me.

It's so nice to have dinner at home!

After dinner, we watched TV and then Mike helped me go to bed. As I lay there, I thought, *there's no place like home,* and then I thought about the three part-time nurses that I would have to take care of me while Mike was at work. I thought some more, *I wonder what they'll be like,* as I drifted off to sleep.

Thirty-Three

Life at Home!

When I awoke Monday morning, I heard the shower running. Mike must be up. Lying in bed and listening for other noises, I wondered if "the nurse" had gotten here, yet. I wonder what she'll be like...probably an old drill sergeant with short, curly gray hair, wearing a nurse's cap and uniform. Soon I heard voices. *The nurse is here. I hope she's nice!*

Quietly Mike tiptoed in. Noticing I was awake, he asked, "Do you want to meet one of your nurses?"

Anxiously, I nodded my head.

He said, "Okay," as he motioned her to enter. "This is Kitty and this is Laura."

I nodded, as she said, "Hi, Laura."

Mike said, "We have a friend named Kitty. Right, Laura?"

I nodded.

She walked toward me and I got a better look at her. *She's not old! She looks fairly young, and she has brown hair and glasses.*

Because the room was somewhat dark, I didn't notice what she was wearing until she came close and asked, "Do you want to stay in bed?"

I nodded. *Oh, my! No uniform! She's wearing blue jeans and a sweater. Why, she's an ordinary human being!*

She said, "I'd stay in bed, too, if I had the chance. It's still dark out," looking at Mike and snickering. "It's early."

"No, it's not," said Mike. "In fact, it's late." Looking at his watch, he continued, "It's already 7:00 am. Usually, I leave at 6:00.

Kitty said, "Oh, my," rolling her eyes and holding her heart as if she were in pain. "That's early. Isn't it, Laura?"

I nodded yes.

Mike said, "I'd better be going soon. Laura, make that sound when you want someone to notice you."

I made a soft, "Ahhhh," sound.

Kitty said, "Oh, I don't know if I'll hear that. Do you have a bell?"

Mike said, "Yeah," rushing off to get it.

The ringing of the bell got louder as Mike approached the bedroom, and he handed it to Kitty. She rang it saying, "Oh, I'll be sure to hear that. How about if I leave it on the bed by your right hand?"

Again, I nodded.

"I'll be out in the living room and I'll leave the bedroom door open. When you want to get up or need anything, just ring the bell. Okay?"

Nodding my head, I thought, *Thank goodness she isn't like I had imagined.*

They left and I went back to sleep. In a few hours, I woke up and rang the bell. Kitty came within a few minutes asking, "Do you want to get up now?"

I nodded. Rolling over on my side, I pushed off with my good hand while she swung my legs over the edge of the bed. As I sat up, I waited a few minutes so I wouldn't get dizzy. She asked, "Do you have to go to the bathroom?"

I nodded my head.

"I'll put your slippers on you while you go to the bathroom."

When I was ready for our walk to the toilet, I sat up straight waiting for her to grab my arm, to count 1-2-3, and to boost me up while I pushed off the bed.

When I was up, as she handed me the cane, and I dropped it. I couldn't bend over to get it. She picked it up and handed it to me. As we walked out of the bedroom, I thought, *cane forward, bad foot first, and then the good foot.* Slowly, we went into the bathroom, and I stood by the commode. She pulled down my pants while I held onto her and then she lowered me to the toilet. I had the addition on the commode (the toilet riser), but even with that, I couldn't get up by myself. *I'll be able to one day soon.*

We walked into the dining area and I went to sit down in a chair. As I reached for my cane, it fell again.

She picked it up again and said, "Oooh! This blasted cane! Now, what should I do with it?"

I shrugged my shoulders.

She said, "I'll leave it up against your chair, but I hope I don't trip over it."

I had breakfast, took a shower, and got dressed. *Am I ever tired! I need to rest!* Being thoroughly exhausted, I sat on the bed too tired to move. Having all my clothes on, I didn't yet have my shoes or brace on.

Kitty asked, "Do you want to take a nap?"

I nodded and nodded YES.

"Do you want to stay here?"

Again, I nodded while lying down. I didn't even care that my head didn't reach the pillow.

She lifted my legs up onto the bed and asked, "Do you want to scoot up?"

I was so tired, I shook my head. *I feel like a wet noodle!*

She covered me and said, "Here's the bell," putting it near my right hand, "Ring it when you want to get up."

When I awoke, I rang the bell and Kitty helped me up. Now I had the energy to attempt the task of putting my shoes and brace on. She acted as if she were going to do it for me. I mustered a strong, "NO!"

She said, "That came out pretty clearly. I guess you want to put your shoes on by yourself, Okay, okay." laughing and raising her hands as if to surrender. "Okay, I understand," she said nodding. "I'll just watch while you put your shoes on."

My right foot was hard enough to get on, but with determination I was able to get my foot in the shoe. For the shoelaces, Carol, my occupational therapist, put tabs on the laces. These made it easy for one-handed people to keep the shoelaces tight.

When I got to the left foot with the addition of the brace, it was nearly impossible. *Ooh, this brace!*

After trying many times, I just couldn't do it. She asked sheepishly, "Do you want me to tackle it?"

Feeling extremely frustrated, I nodded.

She tried with the brace in the shoe but wasn't able to get them both on. Trying to put the brace on my foot first, she couldn't get the shoe over it. I wasn't much help either because I couldn't push my foot down. "Well," she said laughing, "I can't even do it and I have two good hands."

I motioned and grunted to her that I wanted to try again.

She said, "Maybe between the two of us we can get it on."

I nodded.

After a struggle, we both were able to get them on by putting the brace inside the shoe and using the brace like a shoehorn. Kitty exclaimed, "Finally! What teamwork!"

She helped me get up and into the living room where I sat in Mike's favorite chair. Watching TV, I was soon bored. I needed to get up and walk around. Trying to raise myself, I felt as if lead weights were strapped to my buttocks. I remembered my physical therapist's words from the hospital, 'In order to get up on your own, you must have your head forward.'

Trying that, I felt as if I could have landed flat on my face.

Kitty asked, "Do you want to get up?"

Nodding I thought, *yes, but I would really like to do it myself. …but I can't.*

She asked, "Do you want to go to the kitchen?"

Nodding, *that sounds good.*

We walked to the kitchen and back around the living room twice, and I was exhausted. She led me back to the recliner and I fell into the chair. Kitty congratulated, "You made it!"

My day consisted of exercising, walking, and I rested …a lot. When Mike came home at 6:00 pm, Kitty was relieved of her duties.

The rest of the week went smoothly. The other two nurses were not drill sergeants, either. *They're nice!*

By the next week, I was slowly improving. One day Kitty said, "You know, Laura, I think you're getting better. You do most of the work when standing up."

I do? Well maybe, but I still have a long way to go to complete recovery.

Kitty or one of the other nurses took me to outpatient therapy at Lutheran General, where I had two sessions a week. Each session involved physical, occupational and speech therapies. When we got there, whoever took me would park out front while I waited in the car. They used a wheelchair from the hospital to push me from one therapy to another. By the time I arrived home, I was exhausted!

One day when we came home from a long day of therapy, Mike looked around the kitchen and teased, "Hey, Laura. What's for supper?"

He doesn't think I can do it. Well, I'll show him!

The next day I had one of the nurses steady me in the kitchen while I made supper. In the hospital, I was shown many adaptive devices to help me to use only one hand. Many of these were beneficial in the kitchen.

When he came home that evening, the supper was waiting for him. He was so surprised, he asked, "Did YOU do this?"

Proudly, I nodded my head.

He semi-teased saying, "How about making me some chocolate chip cookies from scratch?"

Knowing that was impossible right now, I shook my head slowly. *Not yet, but I WILL someday soon!*

One day as I was sitting in our recliner in the living room watching TV, one of our dogs was chewing on something.

What's he chomping on? My first inclination was to get up and take it from him. Beginning to rise, I then thought, *oh, that's right. I can't get up by myself! . . . How long will I be like this? Will I recover completely? Can I go back to work soon? I guess I should ask Dr. Round these questions at my appointment next week.*

Next week came, and Mom took me to see Dr. Round. He had last seen me when I was at Northwest Community Hospital, and at that time, I could move only my eyes. Mom and I were sitting in one of the examining rooms when Dr. Round came in smiling. He shook my hand and said, "Laura, it's so good to see you!"

I smiled back.

He went on. "And you're doing so well! You were one sick lady. We didn't know if you'd make it!"

He looked around the room as he asked, "Did you walk in here?"

Immediately I started crying, while nodding my head up and down.

Kindly, he said, "I'm sorry I made you cry. But you didn't use a wheelchair! That's great, Laura! Is that a note in your hand? Do you have some questions for me?"

I handed him the note, and he read it as I continued crying.

He said, "Many of the answers to these questions are up to you. It depends on how you do with your outpatient therapy."

I nodded.

"Do you use the feeding tube in your stomach anymore?" he inquired.

I shook my head.

He asked, "Would you like it removed from your belly?"

I emphatically nodded my head up and down.

He turned to Mom, "Does she use it anymore?"

"No, she was using it to take her pills. Now, she's taking her pills with applesauce by mouth."

Dr. Round looked over at me, and I was nodding my head still.

Without any more fanfare, he got me ready and pulled the tube out. It was that simple. He put a bandage on the small area and grinned, "Now, when this heals, you'll have a second belly button. That's your war-wound from the stroke."

I laughed, braying like a donkey!

The squawking sound that I made surprised him. He just smiled, as he said, "If I can be of any other help to you, just let me know."

Thirty-four

Speech

I had been home about a month and Mom had made an appointment for me at Northwestern University Dental School's Cleft Lip and Palate Institute in downtown Chicago. Ruth, my speech therapist helped to arrange a meeting with Dr. Trost to see if I was a good candidate for a palatal lift.

After a full day of testing, Dr. Trost said, "We came to the conclusion, Laura, that you're a good candidate for the palatal lift."

That's good but I know my soft palate will come back. It's just being slow and lazy!

Mom asked, "What will she sound like?"

Dr. Trost said, "She'll be very nasal and she'll probably have to speak much slower."

Come on, soft palate, move! I know it will come back. It just has to.

After our journey home, Mom said excitedly to Mike, "In about a month or two, they'll start making the palatal lift for her. They say it takes about two months to get it fitted with appointments every week. Isn't that great?"

However, Mike didn't sound too enthused. He had the same thoughts as me. We both thought that someday soon, I'll be able to talk on my own.

The next time I had therapy, I printed to Ruth that I was a good candidate for a palatal lift.

She replied, "Don't look forward to it too much. I don't know how much it will help."

She doesn't have to be concerned about me looking forward to it too much. I'm not really looking forward to it at all. My soft palate will come back on its own!

Christmas time was upon us, that busy time of the year. Dr.Trost called Mike from the Institute asking when I would like to get fitted for the palatal lift. Mike and I discussed it and we decided to wait until after the holidays. He said, "Who knows, your soft palate may come back."

The holidays came and went and still my speech was unintelligible. One morning after walking into the bathroom, I looked in the mirror, opened my mouth and said, "Ahhh," while I stared at the back of my throat. That little blob that hangs down wouldn't move at all as it's supposed to. *I'm tired of NOT being understood! I don't care what I sound like! I want to be able to talk! I want that retainer!*

Between Mike and Mom, they made all the arrangements. One of the nurses started driving me to Chicago once a week to the Cleft Lip and Palate Institute at the Dental School, while I got fitted for the palatal lift. We parked in the parking garage across the street from the Dental School and I walked with my cane by myself. I was very slow. *My walking has to get better if I practice!*

In the construction of the palatal lift, the dentist first made an impression of my mouth. With this, he customized the palatal lift device, fitting it on four of my upper teeth. From my teeth, the device extended flush with the roof of my mouth. At the tip of this extension there is an enlarged bulb designed to lift my soft palate.

After weekly appointments for two months, I was finally fitted for the palatal lift. Sadly, it didn't help my speech at all. I wasn't discouraged, though, because I still was sure that my soft palate would respond soon all on its own.

At the end of March of 1981, I had made significant progress physically, and the nurses weren't necessary anymore. At this point, I hobbled through the house without my cane because I had furniture to hold onto. I still needed my cane when I went outside of the house. Mike helped me re-learn to drive a car, but I stayed in Lake Zurich and the surrounding areas. Although my left arm was totally useless, I did have some tingly feeling in my fingers, which I knew was a good sign. I had hope that one day my left arm would be normal. My goal was for complete recovery, but I knew I was far from it. I was determined to continue to work hard.

All in all, I was fairly independent, and I felt good about myself. However, my speech was still unintelligible. I was wearing the palatal lift, but I still couldn't be understood.

On April 7, 1981 Mom took me to The Cleft Lip and Palate Institute in Chicago. The dentist took the palatal lift back to the lab. After Dr. Trost finished her work in the lab, she put the palatal lift back in my mouth. Mary, the speech therapist came in and said, "Okay Laura. Make the PA - PA - PA sound."

Because I knew Dr. Trost did something special to the palatal lift to help my speech, my constant thought was, *I want to be able to talk!* Trying as hard as I could, I took in a deep breath and said, "PA - MA - MA."

Her eyes lit up, as she said, "Can you do that again?"

I repeated, "PA - MA - MA."

"Alright," Mary cheered. "Last week when you were here I asked you to make the PA – PA - PA sound, but it came out as MA – MA – MA. It was nasal sounding because the air was coming out your nose." She smiled wide at me, as she said, "Today Dr. Trost added denture material onto the bulb that lifts the soft palate, which seems to make it easier for you to make the PA sound. Try again!"

My heart beating, I said, "PA - MA - MA." This time I heard it and started laughing.

While Mary waited for me to calm down, she explained, "The palatal lift is now doing what it's supposed to do. It's making a better seal at the back of your throat!"

Mary excitedly said, "Try PA – PA - PA again."

My heart beating even harder, I tried, "PA - MA - MA." Immediately, I laughed again.

Mary said, "Yes, it IS working!" She was visibly excited, which made me more excited!

That's okay if I have to use a device to help me lift my soft palate! I WANT TO BE ABLE TO TALK!

She continued, "The palatal lift is starting to do its job! That's great!" She had to wait a long while for me to settle down. She went on, "You get the first PA out, and then you run out of breath. That's why the others sound like MA. You can work on this with your speech therapist at home. Let's try again. Say PA - PA - PA!"

Deeply concentrating, I tried again, "PA - PA - MA."

"Laura, did you hear it? This time you said two PAs!"

Emphatically, I nodded my head yes. I was excited to try again. We tried many times, but the best I could do was two PAs!

Mary said, "Great job, Laura! Because you run out of breath, that's why you make the nasal MA sound."

I was so excited! It was finally working! The new and improved palatal lift made a HUGE difference in my speech. Finally, I could talk. I had been speechless – for almost a year.

I eagerly rejoined the world to try out my new voice. If I spoke slowly with the palatal lift, I could be understood maybe 50 % of the time. Without it, I could not be understood at all. I was more than ecstatic!

On the way home on the expressway, I read to Mom as many billboard and road signs as I could. They whizzed by, but I read aloud, "T A K E / T H E / P E P / S I / C H A L / L E N G E." I needed to take one breath per sound.

I spoke slowly, but Mom knew I was taking the Pepsi Challenge! She repeated the phrase after me to let me know she had understood.

I blurted out, "B U M P!"

Mom questioned, "Did you say, PUMP?"

"N O – I – S A I D – B U M P."

"Your b's sound like your p's."

"O / KAY."

It took us about an hour and a half to get home, and I read many more signs.

"I / C . . . / W A . . / T O / T A . . . / T . . . / M .

Mom said, "I didn't get any of that."

Slowing myself, I repeated, "I / C A N / N O T / W A I T / T O / T A L K / T O / M I K E!"

"Pretty soon, we'll be home."

When we pulled into the driveway, Mike's red pickup was there so we knew he was home.

I dragged myself out of Mom's car and hobbled into the house. I shouted as best as I could,

"H O N / E Y / I / A M / H O M E !"

Mike was in the other room, but he scrambled into the kitchen with an astonished look on his face. "Was that you?" he asked.

Beaming with delight, I nodded yes.

"You can talk!! What happened?"

"T H E – D E N. . . – A . . . – N . . . - . . ." I knew I wasn't making any sense. I was so excited that I gestured for Mom to continue.

Mom said, "The dentist added onto the palatal lift, and now she can talk!"

He picked me up and began twirling me around in circles as he exclaimed, "Finally, you can TALK!"

A few days later, Mike and I attended Mark and Nancy's wedding. She decided to have Mike be my partner, and the groomsmen walk down the aisle with the bridesmaids because Nancy knew that this would enable me to lean on Mike the whole time.

At the ceremony, we were just about to walk down the aisle and Mike whispered to me, "Remember hold onto my arm and take it slow, just like in rehearsal." With a teasing smile he joked, "If I trip and fall we'll both go tumbling down."

Nancy's wedding went fine, but one of the bridesmaids fainted during the ceremony. She was fine, but Mom was in the congregation and thought at first it was me.

I was also excited at the prospect of finally being able to talk, especially to Nancy and many of our college friends. I discovered one big problem, though. At the reception, one person could hear me fine when we were talking one-on-one. But when there were two or more people talking, I couldn't make myself heard. And then when the music started, all I could do was nod or shake my head. It reminded me of the days when all I could do was nod or shake my head. Still, I was grateful for every bit of progress I had made. I thought, *there are many obstacles on my journey, but I'm not going to let this one get me down.*

A few days after the wedding, Mom drove me to Lutheran General Hospital for outpatient therapy. My speech therapist was thrilled that the new and improved palatal lift was a success. She said, "Let's get to work."

"O / KAY," I ACTUALLY said to her.

She had me repeat many sentences, after which she said, "We can work on your pronunciation. Repeat after me, Did the dog chase the cat?"

I repeated the question, but all the words had the same inflection. My pitch didn't naturally go up at the end of a question like it should.

She said, "We need to work on your pitch - because you sound monotone. You have unchanging intonation. We'll be able to work on that, in addition to getting you to speak more clearly."

Then I went to outpatient physical and occupational therapy. By the time we got home, I was exhausted, as usual!

THIRTY-FIVE

Did You Say Your Name Was Lila?

The telephone was a scary piece of equipment for me. One evening Mike went over to his boss, Jim's house to paint one of their bedrooms. He told me to call over there when supper was ready, which I did. Jim's son answered the phone, and he thought I was one of his buddies clowning around.

He hung up on me!

I called right back, and he hung up on me again! This happened over and over! Mike heard the phone continually ringing. He packed up and came home. Sure enough, when he got home, he found me in tears.

Many times, I wouldn't know if the person on the line understood me. If that person acknowledged what I said, then I knew I had been understood. But if not, then that listener probably didn't have any idea what I was saying.

Because of these problems during the early days of my therapy, I never answered the phone. Those were the days before answering machines or voice mail. I figured they would call back if it was important.

As my speech improved, I would pick up the phone more and more. Sometimes people would hang up on me, which was disheartening. In fact, once I got so mad when someone hung up on me that I broke the phone. After that, I tried to keep my anger under control. As time went on, I began calling strangers.

One day we needed a plumber to fix our kitchen sink. Searching through the phone book, I found the name of a plumber in our area. My speech therapist told me before I called to write down everything I wanted to say in order that I not forget anything. At this time, I could manage a couple syllables per breath.

After dialing the phone, I swallowed hard. I WAS SO NERVOUS! A man's voice answered, "ABC Plumbing."

Trying to remember everything I learned in speech therapy, I said, "T H I S I S – L A U R A – B A R N E T T."

The man asked, "Who . . . is this?"

"L A U R A – B A R N E T T."

"Are you okay?"

"Y E S – I ' M – F I N E.

"Are you sure?"

"Y E S."

"Did you say your name is Lila?"

"N O – L A U R A."

"Oh, Laura. What is your last name?"

"B A R N E T T"

"How do you spell that?"

"B – A - R – N – E – T – T."

"Wait! What was that?"

"B – A S – I N – B O Y,

A – R,

N - A S – I N – N A N C Y,

E,

T – A S – I N – T O M,

T – A S – I N – T O M."

"What was that?"

I repeated it, but I don't think he got it.

"Give me your address."

"3 6 5 – P E B B L E – C R E E K – D R I V E."

"WHAT? …Just give me the number."

"3 6 5."

"OK. 365. I got the number. What's the name of the street?"

"P – A S – I N – P A U L,

E,

B – A S – I N – B O Y,

B – A S – I N – B O Y,

L – E."

"Huh?"

I said it again.

"I'm not getting it. Can you say it over?"

I paused. …I was running out of breath. I said, "I ' L L – C A L L – Y O U – B A C K."

"You want a Big Mac?"

"N O. I ' L L – C A L L – Y O U – B A C K!"

"Huh?"

"B Y E!"

I had to hang up on him because I was exhausted. As soon as I put the receiver down, I began to wail.

It took me an hour or two to settle down. I had wanted to surprise Mike by calling a plumber by myself. Instead, I called him at work, and he arranged for a plumber to come when he was home.

It took me many years to become accustomed to talking to strangers on the telephone. Now most of them know my name is Laura.

Thirty-six

The Lady of the Scooter

When I was in the hospital, my physical therapist had acknowledged that after a while I might hit a plateau. "Your progress may begin to level off. Improvement can pick up again, but no one knows when or how far it will go."

It seems like that's what's going on with me at this time.

Because I wasn't progressing like I wanted, I felt there was a hole in my life that I yearned to fill. Thinking I needed to rejoin the workforce, I talked to Mike and Mom about getting my former job back in the laboratory of Good Shepherd Hospital.

Mom called my supervisor and arranged a trial run for the following week. It was great to see many of my co-workers.

Then reality struck. I tried to run a blood sample through an instrument for a blood count. I managed to get the top off the test tube with one hand, and I held the blood sample under the aspirator of the blood count instrument. Not having a second hand to push the start button, I felt uncoordinated and clumsy.

That day I found out that it was virtually impossible to do my job with my physical condition. That was very hard for me to internalize. Before the stroke, being able to do my job gave me worth and a purpose. Now, I couldn't even do one of the simplest tasks of my job. I couldn't think about this right now.

The only hope I had at that time was that I needed to recover completely. That is what I actually thought at that time. *All the more reason that I need to recover completely.* That statement was a secret I only shared with myself. My feelings were so volatile that I couldn't discuss this with anyone. If I were to even write it to Mike or Mom, I'd be crying hysterically. Depending on the situation, I was ready to explode in hysterical laughter – or a horrendous crying jag.

Mom suggested I volunteer at Good Shepherd Hospital. I liked the idea, and I began volunteering in the Medical Records Department. Because there was therapy at this hospital, I began having physical, occupational, and speech therapies there two times a week instead of at Lutheran General Hospital. This was a much better arrangement because I could drive myself to Good Shepherd, whereas Mike felt Lutheran General Hospital was too far for me to drive.

On my therapy days, I began by driving to the hospital at 7 am, and had physical, occupational, and speech therapies on the ground floor until 10 am There was an elevator, but I took the stairs because I wanted to improve myself. Therapy was on the ground floor, so I slowly went up the stairs to Medical Records on the first floor and volunteered until 12 noon. If I wanted to have lunch in the cafeteria, I went down the stairs. Because I was in my middle 20's, I had plenty of energy for going up and down the stairs, which was good therapy.

After lunch I went back up the stairs to the chapel on the first floor to practice the piano. The tingly feeling in my left fingers was gone, and I had acquired sensation in them. Nonetheless, my left-hand fingers were very uncooperative. Because my thumb and index finger were tightly curled, I practiced with my right hand and only the last three fingers of my left hand.

In addition to my scheduled therapy, I challenged myself with this one hour long piano regimen two times a week for about two years. Although my right hand was back to normal, my piano practice didn't improve my left hand.

My walking was frustrating, also. Whenever I had a chance to walk, I would. If the weather cooperated when going to the store, I parked far from the entrance, so I had to walk. I would NOT use the handicapped parking unless it was raining. I walked inside the bank instead of using the drive-through. Even after all this walking, my gait still did NOT improve.

When I was in Lutheran General Hospital, if I failed at a task, and I failed at just about everything. I continued to work at it, and soon I would overcome the barrier. At home, I worked on something again and again, and many times I still would be unable to do it. My lack of progress at home was unsatisfactory to me.

Mike's approach to help me move forward was to purchase two machines aimed at building up my muscles. He bought me a three-wheeled bicycle and a rowing machine. I rode the three-wheeled bike all over the neighborhood, and I rowed on the rowing machine while I watched TV in our living room. In addition to the many walks I took every day, I also went swimming once a week. Sadly, my walking STILL DID NOT IMPROVE! It was very frustrating, to say the least.

At times like these, I thought, *why did I have this stroke? Why me?* I believed in God, but I didn't have a relationship with Him. I thought of Him as this hard taskmaster who caused me to have a stroke.

There were days when I was sick of trying, I again thought, *what good does it do me to do these exercises over and over?* I felt like giving up.

Thank goodness that feeling lasted at most 24 hours. At the same time, all of my therapists said that I had reached another plateau, and they discharged me from the therapy program at Good Shepherd Hospital.

Beginning to learn a "new normal" for my body, I realized

that I should give up the piano for a while. No longer needing to drive to Good Shepherd Hospital for therapy, I decided to find a new place to donate my services.

Someone told me about Mt. St. Joseph in Lake Zurich. It is a residence for mentally challenged women. Volunteering there, I felt instant gratification. The ladies were so kind, and they didn't hold their emotions back in letting me know that I was appreciated. I loved it!

In the spring, I joined a stroke club at Good Shepherd Hospital. Years earlier, my speech therapist at Lutheran General Hospital had told me about their stroke club, but she had warned, "Only old people go to it. I don't think you will like it."

So I didn't go. But now I decided to try it at Good Shepherd Hospital anyway. Sure enough, all the members were in their 60's and 70's, and I was in my 20's. But through that club, I learned that age is just a number. We all had a stroke in common, and age didn't matter! I learned how therapeutic it was to talk with people of any age who understood what I've already experienced and what I am going through now.

One of the programs in my new "senior citizens" club was a demonstration of a new mobility vehicle called a scooter. It offered independence, but I did not think it was for me. After trying it out, I still wanted to walk on my own.

Because I was determined to walk by myself, I thought that I would be able to recover completely, and that I would never need a mobility aid like that. I was already using a cane, and I thought that was more than I ever would need.

Not long afterward, I went to the local mall. The store "Just Jeans" was on the outside edge of the mall. Mike hated to go shopping, but he was in dire need of blue jeans for work. I parked outside of the store and hobbled toward the door. It was heavy, and it kept closing on me before I had a chance to go through it.

A salesman came to my rescue and held the door open for me.

When I was through the door, he asked me, "Is there anything I can help you with?"

"YES I NEED SOME JEANS."

I knew right after I said it that he couldn't hear me. I couldn't even hear myself. The music was too loud.

He said, "Could you repeat that?"

I shook my head no. Taking pen and paper out of my purse, I wrote down what I wanted.

That was one of my easier shopping trips. Still, I wanted to be as normal as possible so I used my voice as much as possible.

Usually, I shopped for one or two items at the same store which took me about two to three hours, and I was consistently exhausted afterward. The thought of the scooter kept entering my mind, and the independence I would get from having one.

When a lot of walking was involved, I was very insistent that I wanted to walk. Then I would get so tired and think, *that scooter sure would be nice right now.*

There was a battle raging inside of me. The definition of independence for me was not to count on anyone or anything. On the one hand, I knew the scooter would help me a great deal by saving my energy. On the other hand, I had some questions about it. Could I manage it by myself? Would it fit into our car? Could I take it apart and put it together with only one hand?

When I got home from one of the mall excursions, again totally exhausted, my reservations about getting a scooter broke down. I called the salesman, and he came over one night while Mike was home. The salesman brought a brand new scooter with him.

He showed me how I could take it apart by myself and put it together. He also showed me how I could fit it into the trunk of our car and take it out BY MYSELF.

When I took it for a test ride, I could feel the wind blowing through my hair. I said to Mike, "This is great!"

He said, "You can leave it in the car or the garage. It will be here, if you need it."

I ended up getting the scooter. It did give me a feeling of independence but on my terms. I could choose to use it or not. Not wanting to rely on it, I wouldn't use it in the house. It stayed out in the garage or in the trunk of my car.

The definition of independence was changing for me. The moment I bought the scooter, independence still meant not counting on anyone, but the ANYTHING part had changed! The scooter was an inanimate object, not a person, and it was okay to use to help me.

Thirty-Seven

Kids and a Grandpa

Throughout the early post-stroke years, Mike and I tried to have a baby. After going to several fertility specialists, we were still unable to conceive.

At the time, this thought came to me: *I know God is the giver of good gifts. I guess He doesn't want me to have a baby!*

My best friend, Nancy and I were each trying to have a baby at the same time. Then one day, she called me, "Laura, guess what? I'm pregnant!"

Trying to sound excited, I said, "Congratulations," but I was really thinking, *why couldn't it have been me?*

I continued my one-sided dialogue with the God I didn't know: *Don't I deserve a baby? How could you, a good God, not compensate me with a baby? Even after all that I went through, and am still going through!*

With no baby in sight, Mike and I tried the adoption route. We entered a "baby lottery," but sorry to say, our number was not drawn.

I then talked to Mike about our becoming foster parents. If I wanted to take in kids, he wanted that also. We needed to go to a training class, have a caseworker make sure our home was appropriate, and have a background check which included getting fingerprinted.

When that was done, we were ready for our first foster child. We picked up Greg in January of 1985. He was a five year old boy staying at a mission in Chicago because his parents didn't want him. He had no toys and only the clothes on his back. After we picked him up, our first trip was to a department store where we bought him some clothes and a few toys.

Greg was a nice boy when Mike was around, but he was a little devil when alone with me. The caseworker said that he was a menace with women because his mother was only 16 when she had him, and he treated her like a sister. Because of this, he wouldn't listen to me at all. When I told him to do something, he ran away and laughed. It was a big game for him because I could not chase after him. The caseworker coached me to use positive reinforcement. That did work, but it took about a year.

Mike took a job in Elgin, Illinois, which is about 25 miles from Lake Zurich. Not long afterward, he was involved in a car accident. He didn't get hurt, but he did total his truck. In order to cut down on his commuting time, we thought we should look for a house in Elgin. We found one and moved in.

Because the house was larger, we had room for a piano, which I really wanted so I could practice with my left hand. Mike suggested I look in the paper for used pianos in our area, and a few days later we went to a warehouse that had many pianos and other furniture. We picked out a nice used upright piano with a good tone, and it was delivered the next day.

I was so excited to start again on my piano therapy that I went out and bought a book of piano music with a simple left hand part. Practicing a little every day, I hoped that this would help me regain some of the use of my left hand. After about a year, I saw NO improvement. None, whatsoever! My music still sounded labored and halting. It didn't flow!

Back when I was in high school, playing the piano was a form of stress relief for me. I could play the piano and not think about what I was doing. Sometimes my mind would be far away, and the beautiful sounds of the piano would relax me.

In 1986, trying to play the piano with my left hand was a stress producer. Even when I played with only my right hand, my music sounded empty and cold.

One day one of the caseworkers asked me if we would be interested in a 15-month-old boy. The thought struck me immediately, *I would love to have a baby in our home!*

"Can you tell me more?" I asked. I was ready to discuss a baby with Mike when he came home.

"His name is Danny," the caseworker said. "The father and the mother were never married, and Katie had the baby alone. The Department of Children and Family Services were called because she was neglecting him, so they took her baby away until she turns 18, which will be in six months."

As soon as Mike got home, I greeted him with the question about taking in a baby into our home. He was as enthusiastic as I was. I called the caseworker right away and gave her a resounding, "Yes."

In the next few days, I went to garage sales and got many good buys on a stroller, high chair, changing table, some clothes and toys. Mom gave me a playpen and a crib. They were still in good condition even though they had been used for me as well as for some of my brothers.

Danny was such a sweet baby. He could walk, but he didn't mind when I put him in a stroller to take him to stroke club meetings in Elgin. He was content sitting in the stroller for our hour long meetings. As long as he had a bottle, he was happy. Even when the bottle was empty, he enjoyed sucking on the nipple. Greg was in school during these meetings.

Though Danny was a good baby, he was still a physical

challenge. I couldn't grip his body with my left hand. If I placed the fingers of my left hand around his arm by using my right hand, I was able to lift and pivot him wherever I wanted to put him. Because I wasn't able to carry him, the stroller became his mode of transportation whenever he was with me.

Danny's Mom, Katie truly loved her precious little boy. One sure sign was that she corrected the situation which caused her to lose him. She showed the authorities that she was responsible when she acquired her own apartment, and she was always home for Danny's visits.

The day Katie turned 18 was a happy one. I pulled up to her apartment with Danny, and she ran out to the car. She immediately took him out of the car seat, hugging and kissing him. He was happy to see her, but somehow he knew that he would never see me again. Holding both arms out to me, he cried a little as he looked lovingly at me. I reached out for one of his hands and kissed his head. It was a bittersweet moment for me!

Quickly, I got in the car and drove away. Managing to hold the tears back until I got a block away, I stopped and let them flow. Surprisingly after only five minutes, I composed myself and continued home. From this experience, I knew that having a baby wouldn't work out for me. Yet, I was thankful for my experience with him because among a galaxy of twinkling stars, he was a brilliant Alpha Centauri – a super star!

I was sad about losing Danny, but soon, to take his place, we gained a foster grandfather. That's right, a grandpa! Herman was the father of Mike's good friend, Jim, the best man in our wedding. Herman needed a place to stay because his wife had died and he was struggling to make it on one income.

We had an additional family room, and that is where we had kept Danny's playpen. Since we no longer had Danny, this would be the perfect room for Herman, except that it lacked privacy because it was open to the kitchen/dining room. Thinking creatively, Mike came up with the idea of getting a room divider so that the two rooms could be separated. He ordered an industrialized curtain, installed it, and Herman moved in.

Herman helped me with grocery shopping and he even cooked supper once in awhile. Because he was retired, he visited his relatives in Wisconsin for months at a time. When he was around, he would help both of us with anything we needed, as he was able. He was a nice supplement to our mix of a family.

As Greg adjusted to our family, the caseworker began talking to us about possibly adopting him. We both said yes. He was turning into a nice little boy. Then the caseworker talked to Greg's parents about terminating their parental rights, and that's when they came out of hiding.

Just about every weekend after that we met at a public place in Elgin, and the mom and dad would take Greg to Chicago for the day or week-end. They would be punctual whether they picked him up or brought him back. We went to court, and Greg was reunited with his parents.

In addition to providing traditional foster care, plus a home for a grandpa, we were in an emergency teenage run-away program. This entailed taking in run-away teens for a maximum of three weeks.

The first teenager we had was Tammy, a 15 year old run-away. She made it perfectly clear that she did NOT want to go back home. Her parents were divorced and when she lived with her father, he beat her. Her mother, entertaining a bevy of boyfriends, didn't have time for a daughter.

Tammy stayed with us for the allotted three weeks, and then she went to court where it was determined that she would go to another foster home. She wanted to stay with us, but we were a temporary home for her.

At that time, through the traditional foster program, we took in a 13-year-old named Mike. We decided to call him Michael so there wouldn't be any confusion with Mike his foster father.

Back when Michael was six months old, his parents abandoned him, and he lived in a boys' home for many years. Because of these events in his young life, he had many security issues. He went to a school for behavior-disordered children. Primarily, he was a good boy, but very needy, pestering me to give him my constant attention.

Soon we took in two girls who were half-sisters, Lynn, age 16, and Teresa, age 10. They had been placed in ten different foster homes in four years because Lynn had trouble getting along with the children already in the home. In order to keep the sisters together, Teresa had to move with Lynn. They were both good kids, and they were very close to each other. They seldom argued.

On January 9, 1988, our foster grandpa, Herman married Dorothy. Mike and I, and the three kids, Michael, Lynn, and Teresa went to the wedding. The newlyweds lived in Elgin and would come over quite often. The kids didn't lose their foster grandpa, but they gained a foster grandma.

Life was good when we had a revolving door on our home. I was busy being a wife and a mom.

Thirty-Eight

The Cat with Nine Lives

I felt like I had a void in my life, and I didn't know how to fill it. All I knew was that I needed to make better use of my time while the kids were in school. There was a community college about five miles away that interested me. While taking a course about foster children, I learned that the school had a tutoring program. I thought, *I've always enjoyed writing, but I don't know grammar and punctuation as well as I'd like. Maybe I could have an English tutor help me write.*

It was 1987, and the head of the tutoring department at Elgin Community College assigned me to Betty. She was a fascinating 75 year old woman who was a retired college English teacher. She went swimming at the local YWCA, and she had numerous stories of her many travels. This, along with her looks, made her seem much younger than her 75 years. She had an infectious quality about her, which encouraged me to write.

My writing gave me something to do while the kids were in school, and I really liked it! I would drive myself to college with my scooter already in the trunk. When I got to the school parking lot, I would take all of the pieces of the scooter out of my car, assemble them, and I would be on my way.

When it was time to leave, I rode the scooter out to my car, climbed out of it, and took it apart near the trunk. It was harder to work against gravity to move the base of the scooter from the ground up to the car. I took pride in doing it all by myself! It was difficult work, but I really felt independent.

After a couple of years of disassembling and reassembling the scooter, I took the bus instead of driving my car. It was much easier! The bus had a hydraulic lift. All I had to do was drive the scooter onto the lift, and the driver pushed a button to raise me to the level of the bus.

The articles I wrote were non-fiction, usually about some aspect of having to deal with a stroke. The editor of *Stroke Connection Magazine* would print some of the articles, and I would receive copies of the publication as payment for them.

Mike saw that I was writing in cursive. At the college, I occasionally used one of the electric typewriters. Either way, my approach to writing took me a long time. One day, Mike told me about a word processor. My response was quick. "I don't need that!"

Mike gave me a Brother Word Processor for Christmas anyway. It made writing much easier. It was great!

With Betty's help, I was now writing in more detail about what took place when I was in the hospital with my stroke. It was therapeutic for me to write it all down, but it wasn't easy. In some ways I felt like I was reliving the whole hospital scene. I would cry for hours while I was writing things down. Even though it had been seven years since the stroke, I still could hardly believe it had happened.

On many nights, I would wake up in the middle of the night with an idea, or I would remember some incident that took place while I was in the hospital. Being wide awake, I would go to the word processor to write it all down.

One night about 2 a.m., I woke up. Mike was asleep, but I was wide awake. Trying not to disturb him, I went directly to my word processor. I put a piece of hard candy in my mouth. Almost as soon as I put it in my mouth, I swallowed it and it got stuck in my wind-pipe. I could still breathe, but I was gasping for air.

Trying to stay calm, I staggered into the kitchen and wrote on a piece of paper for Mike, "I swallowed a piece of candy." I walked down the hallway to our bedroom and banged the door open with my cane, and then I quickly turned on the light.

Mike flew out of bed. "What? What is it?" I handed him the note. He read it and then started patting me on the neck, frantically asking, "What do I do? What do I do?"

I couldn't talk, so I sat on the bed. Continuing to choke, I shrugged my shoulders helplessly.

He went to the phone in the kitchen and called 911. They began telling him how to do the Heimlich maneuver. In the meantime, I tried sticking my fingers down my throat to see if I could grab the piece of candy. Unfortunately, I wasn't able to get a hold of it, and I swallowed it. I gulped hard, and it scraped my throat as it slithered down. I called out, "Mike!"

When he heard me call, he knew right away that I must have dislodged the candy somehow. He hung up, ran back into the room, and asked if I was okay.

Nodding, "Now my throat hurts," as I rubbed my neck near my throat.

He exclaimed, "You're like a cat with nine lives!" I'm just glad you're okay!"

Thirty-nine

The Day I Threw Bricks

I became intrigued with an Episcopal Church in Elgin not quite a mile away from our home. The sign read St Hugh of Lincoln Episcopal Church. From the outside, the church looked small and homey. It was appealing to me because it reminded me of a good place to raise a family. In its small size, St. Hugh was totally different from the churches I had attended as a child. The different Catholic Churches I went to were mostly large churches.

I looked up the name *St. Hugh of Lincoln*, and he appealed to me too. He lived in the 1100s and wasn't afraid of scolding King Henry II when Henry was trying to make money off the church. Bishop Hugh also worked hard to protect Jews from persecution. I learned that he loved animals and had a pet swan that followed him everywhere. It even stood watch over him while he slept.

I went to St. Hugh for the funeral of a friend of ours in December of 1988. There was a luncheon afterward, and Father Wagner, the Vicar of the mission, invited everyone who attended to come any Sunday for the service.

I thought, *I want to go sometime soon. Maybe this spring!*

When I told Mike about the church, he agreed. He said, "The springtime would be a good time to start going."

I also told the foster kids we had at that time, Lynn, Teresa, and Michael that I would take them in the coming spring. I felt that it was important for them to go to church because it would help them adjust to their new surroundings. So it was really more for social and family reasons, rather than spiritual reasons, that my heart was drawn to church.

Spring of 1989 came and I reminded Mike that we had agreed to begin attending church. "Do you want to go to church at St. Hugh this Sunday?" I asked.

"No, not this Sunday. I have so much to do, maybe next Sunday!"

So I didn't go either.

The next Sunday came, and I asked him again. He said, "Oh no. I have to clean out the garage and the grass needs to be cut. Maybe next Sunday."

Again, I didn't go.

The third Sunday morning, I told Mike that I was going to take the children to church. I asked, "Do you want to go to church with us?"

He said, "Okay."

I gave him a big hug. "Wonderful!" To myself, I said, *now with Mike along we can at least LOOK like a family!*

Except when I went out to the garage and found Mike, he announced that he had changed his mind. "I don't really want to go to church."

I was completely thrown off guard. Instantly, anger hit me. I felt like I was burning all over. I wanted to say, *how dare you change your mind when I have my hopes set so high for a "normal" family? Who do you think you are playing with my emotions like that?*

I was so furious that not one word came out of my mouth. My legs started shaking, and I was afraid I'd collapse. I sat down on the garage floor before I fell down. I had such grandiose thoughts of our "perfect" family going to church, and now Mike was ruining everything.

I looked around for something to throw at him. That's when I saw the bricks. Picking one up, I threw it at him as hard as I could, but it only traveled about a foot. My aim was faulty, and the brick was too heavy for me. Still I kept throwing more bricks, trying to hit him!

I threw another, and another, getting closer, and soon he was jumping out of the way. He laughed nervously, but the bricks weren't even coming close to him! At first I don't think he thought I was serious, but after I threw a few bricks at him, he could tell that I was furious. If I hadn't been so enraged, I would have been laughing hysterically at myself. But this was no laughing matter. I was livid.

Managing to get myself up off the garage floor, I got into the driver's seat of the car. Just then, the kids came into the garage, not knowing what had just happened. They climbed into the car, and we drove away. Mike watched us go.

When we were sitting in the church sanctuary, I couldn't concentrate on the service. All I could think about was what had happened that morning. Going over and over it in my mind, I couldn't believe that Mike had gone back on his word. I was so angry with him!

When we got home, Mike was in the back yard, cutting the grass. He didn't even know we were home. At first, when he came into the house, I avoided him. Then when I was in the bedroom, he came in to change his shirt. He asked, "Do you want to watch *Quincy* on TV tonight?"

I nodded yes as I thought, *he's going to pretend he doesn't even remember what happened earlier!* Thinking about talking to him about the incident in the garage that morning, I felt like I might burst into tears. I didn't want to do that. It certainly was no fault of mine! HE is the one who said he would go, and HE is the one who decided NOT to go! He should apologize to me!

My inability to control my crying had not changed much since I was in the hospital. It was still difficult to manage, and it was obnoxious and loud just like my laughter. At this point in my recovery, I could talk and be understood most of the time, but when I cried I couldn't be understood AT ALL. Then to make matters worse, I couldn't stop after I had started. Sometimes it took me more than an hour to settle down.

Because of this problem with crying, I didn't pursue the issue any further with Mike. We both pretended and continued on with our routines as if nothing had happened.

Despite the conflict with Mike, I was determined to take our foster children to church. My belief was that going to church as a family represented unity, especially between husband and wife. The problem was that Mike's values were different from mine, and I was going to have to get these children involved in church by myself. I felt it was my duty as their foster mother to take them to church.

After that, the children and I went to church just about every week without Mike. There were many Sundays when I told myself I was going to listen especially to the Scripture readings, and then I would end up daydreaming. This happened over and over. Gradually I began to listen and soon I looked forward to going to church. I liked what I was hearing. It seemed that God was beginning to touch my spirit.

Forty

The Changing of My Heart

"I'll just keep a copy in a safe place for future use."

I said this to Mike after I finished the first draft of my manuscript. In my "book" that I called, *How Humor Healed Me,* I had written all about my stroke and the time I had spent in the hospital. I let family and friends read it. I had a great feeling of accomplishment! I put it aside thinking, *maybe someday, I will finish it!*

Being from a musical family, music was always very important to me. Whenever I listened to it, if I liked the arrangement and the beat, I liked the song. One day I was searching the television channels and came across a Christian station playing music videos. I was mesmerized! It played songs from new Christian artists, and the lyrics made my heart leap for joy! This was one of the first times when the lyrics meant more to me than the musical interpretation.

One day I was listening to a discussion on Moody a Christian radio station in my car. It was December, and the announcer was asking his radio listeners to phone in their answer to this question, "Should children be told the true meaning of Christmas?"

My thought at the time was that if we told children that Christmas was about Jesus and His birth, *it would spoil Santa Claus for them!*

A listener called and shared her experience. "I used to think that Christmas was all about the presents, parties, decorations, and music. Now I know it's all about the Christ child. He's God's greatest gift to the human race. He was born of a virgin in Bethlehem. He lived a sinless life. He came to die on a cross for your sins and mine. Then He rose from the dead. He's alive today! Jesus is the reason for the season!"

The announcer pursued his original question, "What should we tell kids about Santa Claus?"

The caller replied, "I have one daughter who is two years old. I want her to know the truth that Jesus Christ is the Son of God, and that Santa Claus is made up!"

That seemed to make sense. My thinking was beginning to change toward the ways of God versus the ways of this world.

All of my frustrations forced me to think about my progress in healing. It had been about 10 years since the stroke, and I had grown used to being able to use only one hand. My gait was slow and arduous, but at least I could walk. I was appreciative I could talk and eat. I began to thank "the Lord" for the many blessings I did have. I was starting to have a grateful attitude.

The following weeks of the New Year, I found a Christian radio station that played contemporary Christian songs. When Teresa came home from school and did her homework in the kitchen, I turned it on the radio. She would hum along with it, and sometimes she would say that she liked a particular song.

One night when we were in the kitchen, I began to explain to Teresa how a specific song impacted me. Suddenly, I had a stinging sensation in my throat. I was about to cry! Abruptly, I distracted myself and changed the subject.

What was curious was that this happened whenever I tried discussing anything about God with anyone, whether they were a

Christian or not. I would always have the feeling that I was about to cry! It had me thinking, *I don't understand what is going on with me. It must be the stroke!*

Mike and I had grown weary of being foster parents. We had taken in 15 foster kids over a period of five years from 1985 - 1990. Because we were in a teenage runaway program, we had the teens anywhere from one night to three weeks. We had the children from the regular foster program for approximately six months to three years each. I had mixed feelings when the children either went home with their birth parents or to another foster home. When certain children would leave, I was sad to see them go. However, there were other kids I was happy to see leave. Whatever the case, we were done with being foster parents.

At that time, the only child we had living with us was Teresa, age 14. We had had her since she was 10, and she was adoptable. She was a joy to have with us! She shared with me that she wanted us to adopt her.

There was no question about it. We loved Teresa, and if being adopted made her feel more a part of our family, then so be it. We went to court, and we adopted her!

That was when she informed us that she wanted to be called Terri. She was now Terri K. Barnett, our daughter!

In May of 1991, someone from Canine Companions for Independence (CCI) in Delaware, Ohio called me to say they had a service dog for me. I had been on their waiting list for two years, and so I was more than excited that my time had come. Mom and I flew to Columbus, Ohio, rented a car, and then drove to Delaware, Ohio so that I could train with my dog at the North Central Regional Training Center.

For the first few days, we trained with the dogs they had at the center. Then the trainers picked a dog for me. My dog's name was Jabba, and he was wonderful! He was a beautiful golden retriever and exceptionally large. We went through two weeks of training together. I learned that Jabba could respond to 40 commands. He could assist me on my scooter, turn off lights, pick up dropped keys, open a door, push buttons for elevators or automatic doors, and even assist with carrying money, receipts, and packages. He COULD do all these things for me, but I didn't need him to do them all. We concentrated on what area I needed the most help.

On top of all this, Jabba became an ice breaker. People rushed up to me to pet him! On the whole, people were very courteous, which I appreciated. They would ask me if it was okay for them to pet him. Soon the topic of the conversation went from him to me. I didn't feel like a 'loner' anymore!

He was also an important social support. He accompanied me to church along with Terri. Jabba also became my cane because I used him for support when I walked. Terri even called him her younger brother! He was like a brother who couldn't talk. Yet the unconditional love that he showed me became a theology lesson. Thanks to Jabba's love toward me, I was beginning to understand God's love for me.

Christian Radio and a dog were helping me grow spiritually! But let's not leave out the TV! There was a Bible program on satellite television that I began to watch on a regular basis during the day.

One day the television pastor was talking about two brothers, Cain and Abel, from Genesis 4, who followed different careers. Able became a shepherd, and Cain worked as a farmer. When it was time to sacrifice to the Lord, Cain offered crops from his farms while Abel offered portions of lamb from his flock.

For some reason – we aren't told – God loved Abel's offering, but he hated what Cain offered. (Maybe it had to do with their attitude.) Cain was furious, and he asked Abel if he wanted to take a walk outside. Genesis goes on to say,

> Now Cain said to his brother Abel, "Let's go out to the field." And while they were in the field, Cain attacked his brother Abel and killed him.
> Then the LORD said to Cain, "Where is your brother Abel?"
> "I don't know," he replied. "Am I my brother's keeper?"

The pastor looked at the audience and said, "Oh, yes, you are!"

That comment shocked me! He went on to say, "You'd better believe that you are your brother's keeper!" He paused, "We live in a country where people are out for themselves. A growing number of people don't care how they get to the top. In the Christian community it should be different. As Christians, we should be concerned about what our brother or sister is doing. Everyone is our brother or sister! They could be our neighbor, co-worker, or friend. He or she could even be our enemy. I don't mean that you should be obnoxious or nosy, but you should have their best interests in mind."

The program went on, but I couldn't get it out of my mind. I thought, *everyone is my brother? . . . hmm. Could that be right?*

My heart was getting more and more tender!

When Terri was a sophomore in high school, we had a German foreign exchange student stay with us for ten months. Her name was Petra Ivana Herlt, but she went by Ivi. She had a disease called osteogenisis imperfecta, brittle bone disease, which caused her to use a wheelchair at school.

When Ivi first came and started school, she was very homesick. She would call home and cry the whole time.

One day she was talking to her mom, and I could tell she had resolve in her voice as she hung up. “Laura, my mom told me to trust in God, and that’s what I’m going to do.”

I recognized the fortitude in her, and I agreed with her as I said, “Alright!” I rallied her on with a fist wave.

From that day forward, Ivi’s spirit improved, and the two girls were a double joy to have around. Ivi played the flute and was involved in the band. Because she was in a wheelchair, she had Terri sit with the band during basketball games to help her.

Ivi’s stay was a good experience for all of us at the Barnett household but especially for Terri.

During Christmas, 1993, there were many nights I would wake up and be wide awake. Going into the living room, I would turn on Moody Christiab radio and lie down on the couch. Mike Kellogg, the overnight announcer had such a soothing voice. He played mellow music and between songs he would talk about God’s love. It was so calming. It made me meditate on God’s purposes for my life. I felt peaceful and soon I would fall asleep.

One morning Mike got up about 6 am, which was his usual wake up time. He walked slowly down the hallway, and as he passed the living room, he saw me on the couch and noticed my eyes open. With a concerned expression on his face, he asked, “Are you okay?”

“Yes,” I said, “I couldn’t sleep and I didn’t want to wake you up.”

While Mike took a shower, I thought about what I should say to him regarding the changes that were occurring inside of me. I was so nervous!

When he was ready to leave, he came into the living room. He gave me a kiss and said, "I'll see you later!"

I said, "Wait . . . Mike. Ah . . ." I didn't know what to say, and I had that feeling like I was going to cry.

"What do you want?" He said, as he was in a hurry, "I have to get to work!"

I waved him off saying, "Oh, never mind."

"Okay, I'll see you later."

I thought, *there must be something special to this message that I get all choked up. I can't think about this now or I will start crying.*

At the time, I happened to be on the board of a small non-profit organization. As a board member, I saw a part of me that seemed to express some of the new lessons I was learning from God's Word. The executive director was showing favoritism toward some of her employees. I'm not good at confrontations, so I tried to talk to her in an easy manner. It didn't seem to make a difference.

Soon after, I gave the board chairman my resignation letter. To the executive director, I explained in what areas I saw her partiality. I went on in the letter that I didn't want to be part of an organization where the Chief Executive Officer (CEO) treated her employees like that. I also included Scripture from James 2, including these lines:

> My brothers, as believers in our glorious Lord Jesus Christ, don't show favoritism. Suppose a man comes into your meeting wearing a gold ring and fine clothes, and a poor man in shabby clothes also comes in. If you show special attention to the man wearing fine clothes and say, "Here's a good seat for you,"but say to the poor man, "You stand

> there" or "Sit on the floor by my feet,"have you not discriminated among yourselves and become judges with evil thoughts?

The CEO never responded, but I was satisfied because I had shared my new values. Her employees were my "brothers," neighbors, friends, and I really did care about them!

I was becoming a different Laura. Would Mike understand?

Forty-one

When Grace Came Down

On March 1, 1994 at about 10:30 am, I was walking through the hallway of my house on my way to the laundry room, pushing a cart filled with dirty laundry. It was an ordinary day, and I had ordinary laundry to do.

Suddenly, I had to sit down at the kitchen table because I felt peace wash over me like a breeze would if I were outside. BUT I WASN'T OUTSIDE! I got the chills and the goose bumps, and I was stunned by the soothing and comforting sensation. Peace was flooding my heart, the peace that passes all understanding! It was a fantastic feeling, but I was confused by it.

I thought, *what's happening? I feel so peaceful!*

Suddenly, I had the feeling that all of my burdens had been lifted. The worries that I had kept locked inside were gone. All my anxiousness about not improving was GONE! All of my insecurities of what people would think of me were GONE!

Some of what I had been learning from the Bible became clear to me at that moment. I took out my Bible and re-read what Jesus had said to Nicodemus in John 3:16:

> "For God so loved the world that He sent His one and only Son that whosoever BELIEVES in Him will not perish but have eternal life."[1]

I was laughing and sobbing hysterically at the same time. One second I'd be crying uncontrollably and the next I'd be laughing hysterically. I couldn't believe that Jesus had died for me!

Turning to another passage that had become especially meaningful to me as a stroke survivor, I read the promise of Paul the Apostle's words in 2 Corinthians 5.

> "Now we know that if the earthly tent we live in is destroyed, we have a building from God, an eternal house in heaven, not built by human hands. Meanwhile we groan, longing to be clothed with our heavenly dwelling, because when we are clothed, we will not be found naked."

I thought, *when I die, I will get a new body! This body of mine has been through so much, even though I'm only 38. I can't wait to get my new body! Wow!*

In actuality, the whole Bible became more transparent to me. These words from 2 Corinthians 12:10 became completely clear.

> "That is why, for Christ's sake, I delight in... weaknesses, in insults, in hardships, in persecutions, in difficulties. For when I am weak, then I am strong."

Christ's power became completely understandable! Even though I'm weak, because of Christ, I'm a super-hero.

I was totally out of control sounding like a donkey braying, a

---

1 All Scripture references are from the New International Version of the Bible.

fog horn wailing, and an air raid siren screeching all at once. I was amazed and astonished by God's love, grace, and peace.

After about an hour of this I was getting totally worn out. While walking to the laundry room, I had to keep sitting down because I couldn't stop laughing and crying.

Later that afternoon, I was listening to Christian radio again, and there was a pastor talking about a God-shaped vacuum that we all have. I was curious.

He went on, "If your God-shaped vacuum and my God-shaped vacuum aren't filled, then we may try to fill it with alcohol, drugs, sex, relationships, materialism, and more. All along Jesus is saying 'If you fill your life with me, you will be satisfied.' And that is the miracle of miracles! He will occupy that God-shaped vacuum that we all have with Himself, and all of us will be complete."

I wondered, *I have a God-shaped vacuum?*

The radio pastor continued, "If you want anything more than God, then you're trying to fill your God-shaped vacuum with something else, and it doesn't work."

I thought about how I really wanted to have a baby but couldn't. I thought, *did I think a baby would have filled my God-shaped vacuum?*

On another day, I was listening to Christian radio yet again, and there was a speaker talking about how much we are affected by people's opinions.

He said, "Nothing stresses me more than people-pleasing. If I have a problem, first, I go to God in prayer. Second, I search His word for answers, and third, I give it time. How much time? Our time is not God's time. He went on, Regardless of people's opinions, God created you for a special purpose."

My thoughts raced, *what could my purpose be? I don't have foster kids anymore. I love having Mike and Terri as part of my family! I know I'm here for them . . . but . . . what else? Was I created for something more?*

Mom came over a few days later, and she and Mike were on the back deck talking to me about the stroke club I belonged to in Elgin.

Mom asked, "Laura, are there any other people in their 30's there?"

Shaking my head, I said, "No, but there is one woman named Rhonda who had her stroke the same year as me. I think she's just a few years older. She's about 40 or 41."

Mom asked, "Are the rest older?"

"Yes, they're in their 60's on up." I answered.

Mike said, "You're probably an inspiration to them."

"Yes," Mom explained, "they probably look at you and say, 'If Laura can continue on for all these years, I can continue on.'"

I questioned myself, *me? I'm an inspiration?*

A few months passed, and I was growing spiritually by reading the Word, going to church, listening to Christian radio, and watching Christian TV. I had heard on the radio many stories of people who had led self-absorbed lives and something caused them to turn their lives over to God. Because they were new creatures in Christ, they told everyone and anyone who would listen about their experience.

Why am I not like that? What is wrong with me? I don't understand this at all.

Because of my emotionalism, I wasn't able to explain the path and joy of redemption to anyone. I had wanted, on several occasions, to share my salvation experience with Mike and Terri. Just the thought of telling them caused breathlessness in me before I could open my mouth, and I was unsure of what to say. Again, I had that stinging in my throat as if I was going to cry! I could never get the explanation out. With great frustration, I had to keep this Good News all to myself.

The love of God was percolating inside me without my ability to pour it out and share it with others. God's love was flooding deep inside me. My soul was like a sponge floating in the middle of this incredible reservoir, soaking up all that I was learning about God. The only problem was that I kept it all inside.

As I look back on March 1, 1994, I see it as the day when God's grace came down on me, and I was forever changed! But I couldn't tell anyone about it! I kept it all to myself.

Forty-two

The Harp

After I became a Christian, my heart-felt desire was to talk to God, but prayer was difficult because of the *emotional lability.* Whenever I tried to share with anyone about God, whether he/she was a Christian or not, I had a stinging in my throat. That unpleasant feeling alerted me to change the subject so I wouldn't cry. Though God knew what was in my heart, this inability to talk to Him or about Him without crying was extremely frustrating.

One night I again had trouble sleeping, and I was laying on the couch in the living room listening to Moody Radio. A song came on with the accompaniment of a harp. With excitement, I thought, *maybe I can play the harp!*

Jabba and I went to a Christian Conference for women at Willow Creek Church in Barrington with Marilyn, the priest's wife from St. Hugh. I mentioned my interest in playing the harp, as I said, "I know how to play the piano. My diaphragm is somewhat paralyzed from the stroke, so I can't play any instrument that needs air from your lungs. Of course, one that requires two hands is out of the question. I think I might be able to play the harp with one hand! It's a beautiful instrument!"

Marilyn nodded, as she said, "Yes, it is. You'd be with good company – the angels! Let's both pray about it."

At the conference, Joni Eareckson Tada was the keynote speaker. When I learned of her life through her book, I found out that she is an amazing woman. She became a quadriplegic at the age of 17 when she broke her neck from a diving accident. What is most astonishing about her is that she paints with her mouth. She paints beautiful pictures!

Since Marilyn drove, I have a manual wheelchair just for times like these when I'm in someone's car. When we got to the conference, she found us a couple of seats near the front, pushed me over there, and Jabba lay down obediently at my feet.

After the conference was over, some of the women couldn't believe that a dog had been there the whole time that Joni was speaking, and he didn't make a sound. Many women rushed over to us, "Can I pet your dog? Oh, what a beautiful dog! He is so patient," while they petted him and fawned over him.

When I got home, he had lipstick all over his muzzle!

About a week later, I saw Marilyn at church, and she said, "A couple just joined our church and she plays the harp! In fact, she's a harp teacher. Isn't God wonderful?"

Nodding my head, I thought, *that was really fast!*

Joyce and I met the next Sunday. She brought me over to her house, which was just a few miles away and showed me her music room. She had a baby grand piano, and in the middle of the room was a large six foot majestic harp. Joyce explained, "This is called a Concert Harp. There are smaller ones that I think would be much easier for you to learn how to play. Since you already know how to read music, it's just a matter of learning the harp fingerings and the form with your right hand."

I asked, "Can you play something for me?"

"Yes," as she sat down, straddled the harp, tilted it back, and played a melodious song with harmonies that mesmerized me with their hypnotic tones. She ended the song with running her finger up the harp strings. She asked, "Do you know what that's called?"

Shaking my head, I was so moved by the dazzling music that I could not utter one sound.

"A glissando," she said. "Even though you can only use one of your hands, you will still be able to make beautiful music!"

I just nodded my head, as I was happily anticipating what may be waiting on the horizon for me!

Not long after meeting Joyce, I had an appointment with my gynecologist. She said, "You have a cyst on your uterus that needs to be removed. It probably is benign, but I want to remove it along with your uterus and have the cyst tested. You won't have a complete hysterectomy because I will save your ovaries."

I was scared, and I didn't know what to make of all of this. In the quiet recesses of my heart, I thought, *okay, God, I'm yours. Won't you protect me from more hurts? Why do I have this physical issue after going through so much with the stroke?*

There was no answer.

Before the surgery, Mike and Jabba were in the room with me. Mike put a surgical cap on him, which Jabba kept on as they walked with me while I was being pushed on a gurney to surgery by an aide. By the time we got to the surgical area, we had drawn a crowd. Many of the people were employees, but some were visitors passing by. Jabba was in his glory! He loved the attention of having people look at him and laugh. We said our goodbyes because they could go no further. The surgery went as planned, and I later learned the cyst was negative.

The next evening, Mike was visiting me, and we were watching television. All of a sudden, I hopped up in bed as best I could, as I said, "I hear live harp music."

Sure enough my new harp teacher, Joyce came into my room with her husband, Loren pushing her huge six foot tall Concert Harp on a cart with wheels. She had been tuning her harp in another room. She had on a long formal gown, and Loren was dressed in a tuxedo. I was completely surprised! He played the flute along with her on the harp, and they complimented each other. It was gorgeous! They played a few songs, and I was so relaxed that I closed my eyes and almost fell asleep. After my private concert was over, Mike helped them carry everything back to their car, and I fell asleep dreaming of the angels.

The next day was Sunday and I had expected Mike to bring Jabba and stay with me the whole day. He called that morning, "Laura, I have to get a whole new computer system for work. I can still come to the hospital, but it will probably be late around 6:00 pm."

"Okay," I said a little disappointed.

Noticing my hesitation, he said, "I will come as soon as I can. Anyway, you're coming home tomorrow. Isn't that great?"

"Yes," I said with a smile, as I was happy to be going home soon.

Mike came at 6:00 pm like he said and stayed till 8:00 pm when visiting hours were over. He said, "I'll be here tomorrow afternoon to take you home. Okay?"

"Okay,"I said, "I'll be ready!"

The next day came, we left the hospital, and as I entered the kitchen of our house I gasped as I saw it and was amazed! In a corner of the dining room was a harp that stood about four feet high. I couldn't believe it, as I asked Mike, "What did you do?"

"I rented a harp," he said, "I went with Joyce and Loren yesterday to pick it up at a lady's house near Chicago. That's where I was yesterday when I said I couldn't come to the hospital. We wanted to surprise you. I guess it worked!"

"You better believe it did," I said, as I ran my index finger up the harp strings in a glissando as Joyce had done a couple of weeks ago at her house. "Oh, Mike, this is the best surprise that I have ever had! Thank you," as I gave him a kiss and a hug! "I had no idea!"

Mike said, "You're more than welcome!"

FORTY-THREE

The Miracle

Joyce started teaching me how to play the harp, and she would come over to my house. A previous teacher of hers had printed out for me an arrangement of, "Fairest Lord Jesus" to be played with one hand. As soon as I learned the fingerings and the right form, I set out to learning the music made especially for me. It is such an elegant instrument, and I was on my way to making beautiful music. Soon I was able to play the arrangement of "Fairest Lord Jesus".

Only a few months later, Jabba and I went by bus to the dentist in Chicago for a check-up for my palatal lift. The dentist informed me that she thought my soft palate was coming back. I was astonished! She and the speech therapist showed me with a hand mirror that my soft palate would raise whenever I increased the volume of "Ah!"

I couldn't believe it! I was so grateful to God for giving me this gift! Feeling like I was going to cry, I managed to hold off. Once I got home by myself, I let the tears flow. Going into the bathroom, I looked in the mirror at the back of my throat. I said, "Ah," and when I increased the volume, my soft palate went up higher and higher.

Trying to jump while holding onto the counter, I was laughing and crying at the same time. I felt so loved by God! His wisdom is immeasurable. His blessings are plentiful! Since I was crying anyway, I praised Jesus! I choose to think of this whole episode as a miracle! My faith grew tenfold! It had been 15 years after the stroke, and I was still improving!

In the following years, I'd take the palatal lift out of my mouth when I was in normal conversation, and I'd put it back in for those times when my soft palate needed a little boost. Many years later, I didn't need it at all. It truly is a miracle!

My life since Christ has not been trouble-free. About a year after the miracle occurred, I fell and broke my right shoulder. Mike asked his boss, "What helped you when you broke your shoulder?"

He said, "A hospital bed."

Mike had a hospital bed delivered, and it helped me to get rest at night.

During that time, I was quite helpless. My right arm was bandaged close to my body, unable to be used. Because I needed my right arm for a cane, I couldn't use one, so my mode of transportation was a manual wheelchair. Having only my right leg to help me to get around, I wasn't up for any races.

Because my balance was so bad, Mike and I decided that I should use the scooter in the house. This was 1996 and scooters were not too prevalent.

I asked my orthopedic doctor, "What do you think of me using my scooter in the house?"

He exclaimed, "WHAT! You're going to use a scooter?"

He thought I meant those toys for kids on two wheels.

Mike built a ramp in the garage leading into the house. He would do whatever needed to be done to make my life easier.

Forty-four

Gilda and Grace

My time was almost up with the rental harp, and I was sure I wanted a harp of my very own. Joyce and I discussed the sizes from as small as a lap harp to a big concert harp. I decided on a 22 string lap harp. We ordered it and waited.

My new lap harp arrived and I named her Gilda. Mike gave her to me as an anniversary present, and I began practicing at once. Because it was hard for me to hold Gilda between my legs, Joyce had a solution. A harp bra! It was custom-made by a woman in Chicago, and it looked like a brazier with 2 very small cups that fit into the base of the harp. The strap went around my waist, and clasped together on the side. Now, I could play the harp, and it would stay still.

One day I was practicing, and I wondered if I could play the harp with my left hand. If I brought the harp to my left fingers, I could pluck the strings with two of my fingers. Then, if I stretched out my left thumb with my right hand and plucked a few of the strings, my thumb would relax for a few seconds before it curled back up into the palm of my hand!

At a harp workshop that Joyce and I attended, I found a baby harp for sale. It was an 8 string harp, and it was the perfect size for me to work on my left thumb. There were only a few songs that

I could play with it, but I was determined to get my left thumb to relax. God is so awesome! He knows what we need, and He sometimes gives it right when we need it.

That's all I wanted to do! It was rather boring, but after many months, I was able to use my thumb and two of my fingers on my left hand. Because I wasn't able to hold my left arm up, I had to prop it up with blocks of wood on the armrest of my scooter.

Joyce came over to give me a lesson and I showed her, as I said excitedly, "Look, I can play with two hands!"

She exclaimed, "Yes! What you need is a double-strung harp!"

"What's that? I questioned.

"It's a harp that has two sets of strings, one for each hand. Loren made one from a kit, but we haven't been able to sell it. It's in our basement," she said.

Excitedly, I asked, "Can I try it?"

"Yes," she said, "I'll bring it over next week."

Next week came and Joyce brought the harp over. She tuned it and I was able to use my left hand, but I had to stop and stretch out my left thumb every now and then. Mike and I decided to buy that harp from Joyce and Loren, and I named her Grace because her sound was beautiful and graceful.

Grace was working out so well that I could play the song, "Kum-Bah-Ya" all the way through without stretching out my thumb. Unfortunately, I practiced that song almost every day for over a year, but I didn't improve. I did NOT think I made beautiful music! The song sounded very jerky, and it didn't flow. I had trouble getting my left hand in sync with my right.

Being extremely discouraged, I was renewed with the changes that were occurring in my left thumb! It had been about 20 years post-stroke, and I was still seeing improvement! Granted, it wasn't big improvement, but it was improvement none the less. I had control over my left thumb! Up until I started trying to play the harp with my left hand, my left thumb was tight and stayed hidden in the palm of my hand. I had no control over it while my other fingers would curl around it. But now, I could move it back and forth without hardly any effort at all, and it would stay outside my curled fingers! Any occupational therapist would be stunned at this revelation because now I could easily wash the inside of my hand. I was thankful for every tiny blessing that I received from God!

Joyce and Loren were both retired, and they longed to be near their daughter, her husband, and their three grandsons. Soon Joyce came with the news, "We're putting our house up for sale, and we plan on moving to Idaho."

Everything fell into place, and they moved.

Forty-Five

Tully – Another Service Dog

My life since Christ has NOT been trouble-free. I fell in the kitchen and hit the back of my head on the handle of a cabinet. Later I went to the Emergency Room because I had a non-stop headache. A brain scan showed that a hematoma (a small pool of blood) had developed in my brain causing the headache.

The brain surgeon said, "When you hit the cabinet handle with the back of your head, it caused your brain to rush forward and slam into the front part of your skull causing the hematoma. A little area on your head will need to be shaved. Then I will drill a small hole into your skull to drain the hematoma. Once it is drained, your headache should go away."

In response to the brain surgeon, I just kept nodding my head yes, while I cried. Because I had this headache, my impulsive crying increased. I cried for everything and anything.

The surgery was successful! Because I knew God was with me, I wasn't afraid! When I woke up from the anesthesia, my headache was gone. I praised Jesus!

While I was in the hospital, my doctor ran many blood tests

on me. She said, "An antibody produced in your liver seems to be the cause of your stroke. Most likely, you were born with this antibody."

I finally knew the medical reason WHY I had had the stroke!

Though I slowed down my life quite a bit, I still remained independent. Jabba, too, was beginning to slow down due to his age. He was 12 years old, and most service dogs retire at 10. I needed to get another dog.

In May of 2002, Terri drove me to Canine Companions for Independence in Delaware, Ohio where we stayed for two weeks. I called home every day, but Mike never answered the phone. I thought, *I guess he doesn't want to talk to me!*

It was a wonderful trip, and Terri got another brother who didn't talk back. Tully was a well-behaved black Labrador Retriever.

When I brought Tully home with me, Jabba was jealous! Both of them were friendly with all kinds of dogs, but Jabba would walk far away from Tully as if he had a communicable disease. This went on for about two weeks.

One day, Tully and I were going somewhere on the bus, and Jabba was lying on the couch. In my scooter, I went next to him and said, "Goodbye, Jabba" and gave him a kiss on the head and an ear scratch.

Tully was on a leash connected to the scooter, and when he passed by the couch, Jabba gave him a kiss!

"Oh my, Jabba," I exclaimed! "Is Tully your friend now?"

He had a look of resignation in his eyes, as if to say, "Aw, Tully, you go with her. I'll stay home and rest!"

From that day on, they were buddies. Jabba died eight months later.

Forty-six

Trouble with Mike

My relationship with Mike was declining. BIG TIME! Our love for animals seemed to be the only bond that held us together. We had four big dogs and a half acre back yard that was fenced in for them to run. And run they did! If the weather was nice when Mike would come home from work, he would throw the ball for them and all four of them would take off like a stampede trying to reach it first. In the house, Mike would play hide-and-seek with them. He would close them off in a room, hide, and then I would let them out. They would sniff and look all over for him. Sometimes he would have to call them by name so they could find him.

Even Mike's love for the dogs began to dwindle. He was depressed, and I thought it was because of me. We had a big deck in back, and one summer night he was sitting out back reading the newspaper. Someone was selling an island on the Rock River about an hour from us. He called the owner, and he went a few days later taking Jeff, a buddy from work. He took many pictures, and showed them to me with excitement in his eyes!

It was a five acre island with two cabins on it. The island was right on the Rock River with a small channel encircling the land. Both cabins were very rustic, with the larger, main cabin having plumbing and electrical systems, whereas the smaller cabin only had electricity strung across from the larger cabin. The main cabin had one big living room and eating area with a large wood-burning stove, small kitchen, one large bedroom, and one full bathroom. The small cabin had a fireplace and four regular-sized rooms that could be used in a variety of ways. There was an area around the cabins which was kept mowed, and beyond that were trees and wild brush.

"When can I see it?" I asked.

"I don't know if you can get out there," he said.

"Why not?" I demanded.

"Because it's an island, and we had to take a boat. Jeff and I drove to a park about a mile down the river, and the owner of the island picked us up in his pontoon boat, which he's selling along with the island."

I said, "There MUST be a way for me to get there and see it!"

Mike suggested, "We'll figure out a way."

About a week later, Mike said, "I spoke to John Brada about possibly going in on the island with us. He wants to see it."

John and Mike had worked together. We had been over to John and his wife's house, and they had been over to ours a few times. John and Karen had 3 boys, Danny (age 20), Jeff (age 18), and Christopher (age 13).

Mike said, "The owners said we could use the island and cabins for a week-end to decide if we want to buy it."

Mike and I went out the next Saturday morning with the three dogs, and the Brada's followed. We stopped alongside the island on a busy road, and Mike and John got out to get the pontoon boat. We were parked on a hill, and the guys went down the hill where there was a rowboat. They rowed across the small channel, and then they walked across the island to the pontoon boat, which was tied to the dock. Karen drove her boys in her car to the park, and I drove our car there, which was about a mile away from where we dropped them off.

When I got out of the car it was difficult for me to walk in the grass because it wasn't level like most grassy areas I was used to. When Mike and John got to the river's edge, they loaded up all of our supplies from the cars to the boat. As I leaned against the front of the boat, Mike and John hoisted me up, and Mike helped me walk because the boat was unsteady. As we walked to an open seat, I sat down, and Mike shouted, "ALL ABOARD!"

All the others hopped on the boat and our four dogs scrambled on as Mike let go of their leashes.

We ended up buying the island, and Christopher Brada named it 'Paradise Island'. It became my home away from home! I loved it! God's presence is most evident to me in nature. His handwriting is all over the island! Whenever we were there, I felt as if we were far away from civilization. There were mainly trees along the banks of the river, and most of the cabins or homes were set back unable to be seen from the river.

During the week at our house in Elgin, Mike would hardly talk to me, but on the week-ends with the Brada Family, he was making jokes and teasing me, just like old times.

I thought, *what is going on?*

A few years after we bought the island, Karen and John told us of their plans. An opportunity had come up for John in Florida, and Karen hated the winters in the Chicago area. They found a home right on a channel that led to the Gulf. It sounded perfect for them.

I thought, *with the Brada's gone, I wonder if Mike will ignore me the whole week-end just as he does at our house in Elgin!*

Initially, Mike talked to me while we were at the island. He would even joke and tease a little. This lasted only a few months. Soon he was ignoring me all of the time. I couldn't handle it. I felt like I was going to go crazy. When I asked him a question, many times he would just grunt at me, or answer with a blunt YES or NO.

I couldn't verbalize my problems, even with Tully because of the emotional lability. Tully had a sixth sense, as some dogs seem to have. He would just look at me with those beautiful brown eyes and give me a kiss, as if to say, 'I'm here for you, Mom!'

In October of 2004, I left Mike. I couldn't talk to God about this because of the emotional lability. Tully and I stayed with Mom in her trailer in a mobile home park a few miles from our house. It was far from the perfect situation for me.

First, there were stairs leading into her house, so I had to leave the scooter outside. Mom had a carport, which provided some protection for the scooter, but it wasn't the best scenario to charge it out in the cold because batteries don't do well in cold weather.

Second, Mom was partially blind from glaucoma, and her hearing wasn't good. With my speech problem, that led to some very interesting conversations between Mom and me. Usually if someone didn't understand me, I would write things down. However, that didn't work with Mom because she was legally blind. Sometimes I would call her up on my cell phone from the same room, and she said she could understand me a little better on the phone. Finally, if I cried, she got frustrated because she couldn't understand my speech, and I got frustrated because I couldn't control my crying. It was NOT a good situation!

The priest from St. Hugh Episcopal Church counseled Mike and me. It was only a band-aid covering up a bigger problem that I was totally unaware of. We were separated for 6 weeks. I went back with Mike, and things were pretty good for awhile. I didn't understand what was going on, but I knew the God who holds the whole world in His hands. He knew what was going on, and I was learning how to give all my anxieties to Him.

Again God knew what I needed. He was trying to prepare me for what lay ahead. Nancy and five of my college girlfriends got together for a week-end in February, 2005. We usually get together once/year. Many of them live in down state Illinois. We have supported one another through health challenges, marriage problems, kids, and just the everyday problems of life. For the main part of the week-end, all we do is laugh. I REALLY NEEDED THIS!

What I remember about this particular week-end was that I felt a heavy load being lifted off my shoulders when I told "the girls" about my problems with Mike.

Mike, Tully, and I took a trip to Florida in March, 2005. The plan was that we would drive down to Tampa, Florida, where Mike had a business meeting for a week. The second week was up in the air! We would do whatever we wanted and go wherever we wanted! It sounded exciting to me!

We made it down to Florida, and we stayed at a hotel in Tampa while Mike went to his business meetings. When we were in the car leaving the hotel in Tampa, I excitedly asked, "Well, where are we going to go?"

He said, "I would like to go to Boca Raton, Florida. It's about 250 miles southeast of where we are now, and they have a drug treatment program that I would like to go to. It's called The Watershed."

I heard what he was saying, but it made no sense at all. I responded, "What?"

He said, "I'm addicted to Vicodin, and whenever I stop taking it, I get sick!"

I thought, *no wonder he has been acting so weird!*

We drove to The Watershed in Boca Raton, and Mike checked in while I waited for him in the car. When he returned, he said, "They were expecting me because I had called them while we were in Tampa. Now, we have to find a hotel nearby for you and Tully to stay at."

We found a Holiday Inn three miles away. Mike helped Tully and I get settled, and then he left. My head was in a whirlwind! What just happened? I can't believe this!

On the one hand, I was glad that there was a reason as to why Mike was acting so strange, but on the other hand, this made for a lonely vacation. Thankfully, I had Tully. When Tully was with me, I usually didn't feel alone.

The Holiday Inn was very nice. It offered room service, an outdoor pool, which I took advantage of, and many of the amenities most hotel rooms have. Tully and I kept ourselves busy!

Because Mike was in a structured program, I couldn't see him for the first few days. When I finally could see him, I had to go to him, which was a bit of a challenge because my doctor hadn't renewed my driver's license after the head injury.

I ended up borrowing a manual wheelchair from the hotel, and taking a taxi to the Watershed. When we arrived there, Mike was in good spirits. That day we had many meetings with a psychiatrist, social workers, and caseworkers. Mary, the psychiatrist said, "Mike, you should go to Alcoholics or Narcotics Anonymous (A.A. or N.A.), and Laura, you should go to Al-Anon."

I questioned, "What is Al-Anon?"

She said, "It's a meeting for the family members and/or friends of people who go to A.A. or N.A. It helps them understand what their friend or family member is going through, and how best to help them."

The program at the Watershed lasted for ten days. Mike talked Mary into letting him get discharged from the program after seven days. He wanted to go home and get back to work.

When we got home, Mike went to Alcoholics Anonymous for a few months, and I went to Al-Anon for a few years.

After a few years I fell again, hit my head, and got another hematoma in about the same spot as before. My doctor teased me by saying, "You didn't do it good enough last time, so you had to do it again."

The brain surgeon was the same as the one a few years ago, and he said, "Laura, we're going to have to stop meeting like this."

My recovery didn't go as well as it had before. I was to stay in a power wheelchair and transfer only when absolutely necessary. My legs were never the same, but I hung on to my independence. I also hung on to the fact that God is in control. Knowing that whatever happened, I was under His care.

It was April 25 on Dad's birthday anniversary, when Mom died. Out of seven kids, I only have two siblings in Illinois, and the rest are scattered across the country. One brother we had lost track of for about twenty five years, but he had resurfaced about ten years prior. They all came for Mom's funeral, and it was a tribute to a life well lived! It was a blessing to see her die peacefully. She was 90 years old.

Mike and I separated not long after that, and I moved out. God had told me, not in an audible voice, but in a knowing deep within my spirit. He said in that still, small voice of his, it's time! You have done all that you can. It's time for you to leave.

At that time, Tully and I moved to a retirement home in Elgin. I WAS SO JOYFUL! I was out of that house of oppression. Mike never hit me or verbally abused me, but the SILENT VIOLENCE almost made me go INSANE! Finally, I could talk to and about God without crying! It was so freeing!

Sadly, the retirement home closed down after we had been there a little over a month. I had ten days to find another place to live.

The McHenry Villa Retirement Home had a vacancy. Even though McHenry is only about 30 miles away from Elgin, it's still too far to be able to attend St. Hugh Church and the Stroke Survivors Support Group on a regular basis without me being able to drive a car.

We moved to McHenry Villa, and Tully was a big hit! He was the only dog there, and many of the staff and residents spoiled him. He even earned the title, "King of the Villa."

I trust God to help me with everything, especially my attitude. God consistently gives me a PEACE that passes all understanding, and a JOY that lasts. Happiness, I have learned over and over, is fleeting. It's here today and gone tomorrow. The joy I have now is genuine and durable. That's because it's from Jesus, and it's new every morning.

When I first moved, the Villa had an old donated organ in one of the back offices. In a hymnal, I found many hymns that ministered to my heart, but "God Will Take Care of You," was especially poignant. All of my worries, I give to God!

Mike and I were divorced in April of 2013. He moved out west for a job in the state of Oregon.

Again, I fell not long after the divorce. This time I broke my hip and needed surgery as well as rehabilitation. Throughout this whole ordeal, God got my attention. He inspired me to finish writing this book. I continued from where I had left off. In my spirit, I felt God say,

You already wrote about your hospitalization in 1980. Now, I want you to write about when you got home and up to the present. That part is about ME! I want you to write about MY power and how I redeemed you! Through your story, others can find the LOVE, JOY, and PEACE that I offer, which leads them to salvation!

Tully died not long after I broke my hip, and I had to say goodbye to my trusted helper, companion, and friend. After two weeks of mourning for my Tully Boy, God inspired me to get back to writing where I had left off many years ago.

On September 6, 2015, I was baptized in a nearby lake by Pastor Josh of the Evangelical Free Church of McHenry where I have been attending. It was a very meaningful experience! By going underwater, I publicly express that I have died to sin. I still sin but now I'm aware of it. It no longer has a hold on me. Coming up out of the water, I symbolically demonstrated the newness of life in Jesus Christ.

Since my stroke, I now can see that I kept looking for my purpose in life through activities and endeavors. Being involved in many different groups, I was searching for my purpose in life. My ultimate purpose is found in Jesus Christ. I accept the stroke and all the baggage that comes with it. I thank God for the stroke because without it, I still may be stuck in my sin, and I give God all the glory.

GOD TRANSFORMED MY STROKE TRAGEDY INTO A SPIRITUAL TRIUMPH!

The End

Printed in the United States
by Baker & Taylor Publisher Services